W9-AGY-119

Augustine: His Life and Thought

PANNELL LIBRARY

#635560 1

BR
1720
.A9
.564

60791

AUGUSTINE

His Life and Thought

WARREN THOMAS SMITH

John Knox Press
ATLANTA

Library of Congress Cataloging in Publication Data
Smith, Warren Thomas, 1923-
    Augustine, his life and thought.

    Bibliography: p.
    Includes index.
    1. Augustinus, Aurelius, Saint, Bp. of Hippo.
2. Christian saints—Algeria—Hippo—Biography.
3. Hippo, Algeria—Biography. I. Title.
BR1720.A9S64   281'.4'0924 [B]   79-92071
ISBN 0-8042-0871-9 (pbk.)

© copyright John Knox Press 1980
10 9 8 7 6 5 4 3 2 1
Printed in the United States of America
John Knox Press
Atlanta, Georgia 30365

Acknowledgment

Unless otherwise noted, the Scripture quotations in this publication are from the Revised Standard Version Bible, copyright 1946, 1952, 1971, and © 1973 by the Division of Christian Education, National Council of the Churches of Christ in the U.S.A. and used by permission.

The author expresses his appreciation to Penguin Books Ltd. for permission to quote from *Saint Augustine: Confessions* and *Augustine: The City of God* and to The Catholic University of America Press for permission to quote from *Fathers of the Church*. These important sources are recommended as collateral reading for the study of Augustine.

All quotations from *The Confessions* will be found in R.E. Pine-Coffin, tr., *Saint Augustine: Confessions* (Middlesex, England: Penguin Books, Ltd., 1961). Pp. 21, 22, 24, 25, 28, 31, 34, 37, 40, 45, 47, 55, 58, 59, 60, 61, 64, 65, 68, 70, 71, 72, 73, 74, 75, 76, 77, 78, 83, 87, 88, 92, 97, 99, 100, 101, 104, 107, 109, 111, 113, 114, 116, 118, 120, 124, 125, 126-28, 130, 131, 144, 145, 147-49, 159, 160, 171, 172, 175, 177, 181, 184, 187, 189, 190-92, 194, 195, 197-99, 202-204, 201, 211, 223, 239, 251, 303, 329. Reprinted by permission of Penguin Books Ltd.

All quotations from *City of God* will be found in David Knowles, ed., *Augustine: The City of God*, tr. Henry Bettenson (Middlesex, England: Penguin Books, Ltd., 1972). Pp. xxix, 14, 42, 106, 197, 216, 414, 637, 1027, 1037, 1039, 1091. Reprinted by permission of Penguin Books Ltd.

Quotations from Augustine's *Letters* will be found in *The Fathers of the Church* (New York: Fathers of the Church, Inc., 1951-1956), volumes of Letters I–V. Used by permission.

Quotations from the following are found in *The Fathers of the Church* series and are used by permission of The Catholic University of America Press:

On the Value of Believing	*On the Happy Life*
On the Good of Marriage	*On the Teacher*
Soliloquies	*On the Immortality of the Soul*
Against the Academics	*On Music*
On Holy Virginity	*On the Magnitude of the Soul.*
Retractions	
On Order	

Certain quotations from *On the Trinity* are found in *The Library of Christian Classics* (Philadelphia: The Westminster Press, 1953).

Quotations from the following come from: Erich Przywara, *An Augustine Synthesis* (New York: Sheed and Ward, 1945):

Soliloquies (selected passages)	*Sermon on the First Epistle of John*
Against Julian	*Admonition and Grace*
The Spirit and the Letter	*Letters against the Semi Pelagians*
On Nature and Grace	*On the Psalms*
Sermons	

To My Son

James Warren Smith

"Surely what Cicero says comes straight from the heart of all fathers, when he wrote: 'You are the only man of all men whom I would wish to surpass me in all things.' "

Augustine, *An Unfinished Work Against Julian*, quoted in Peter Brown, *Augustine of Hippo* (Berkeley and Los Angeles: University of California Press, 1967), p. 135.

Augustine

A laughing boy,
He loved columns,
Because they towered skyward.
A passionate youth,
He loved beauty
And lost his way in the clouds.
A learned man,
He found his sky again
And, higher than the mists of midnight,
Built the City of God
With towers that touched the stars.

Earl Bowman Marlatt, *Chapel Windows* (1924)

Preface

Of all figures in Church history, few have been so thoroughly studied, described, and dissected as Augustine. Every aspect of his life and thought has been probed, examined, and scrutinized under the academic microscope. Scholars have explored his tremendous store of ideas; psychologists and psychiatrists have delved into his personality; writers of piety have thoughfully sought to interpret his life of faith.

Why, then, another study? It is my attempt to tell Augustine's story in very simple terms. This is a work designed specifically for a lay readership. Special emphasis is given to the land which produced Augustine—Africa. His roots sank deep in African soil, and the African sun shone upon his head.

I wish to convey my profound obligation to all who in previous years have written about Augustine. It would be impossible to enumerate the many significant works, but special mention must be made of Peter Brown's *Augustine of Hippo* which is "in a class by itself." It has been an ideal guide, for which I am indeed grateful.

I must express my indebtedness to Professors John Lawson and Arthur W. Wainwright of Emory University; the late Professor Richard M. Cameron of Boston University; former President Grant S. Shockley and Professor Kenneth E. Henry of The Interdenominational Theological Center; and Professor Clarence L. Abercrombie, III of Wofford College, all of whom read my manuscript in various stages of its development. For their invaluable suggestions and comments I am immeasurable grateful. Responsibility for the content of the work, I must assume.

Special thanks to my family—Barbara and our Warren, whose patient understanding and supportive interest kept me employed in this awesome responsibility.

In quoting from Augustine, many sources have been used. My aim has been to select the particular translation which best conveys the mood and soul of Augustine, stated in fresh, contemporary figures of speech. Lengthy passages have been reduced. Frequently, phrases have been linked together to form a single paragraph in order to capture Augustine's thought through a minimum of words. I sincerely hope that I have been faithful both to the letter and the spirit of Augustine, and that the reader will catch the vitality of the message. "Faith gives the understanding access to these things . . ." (Letter 137, quoted in Erich Przywara, ed., *An Augustine Synthesis*, p. 65). Most of all, I am indebted to Augustine himself. After years of writing I feel that I have come to know him personally. He is, after all, very real—an authentic individual—an African who was flesh, blood, tears, laughter. My aim has been to make him come alive to the reader. In so doing, it is likewise my hope that along with Augustine I, too, might make my witness to the grace of God as seen in Jesus the Christ. "This then is the first grace of God's gift, to bring us to the confession of our infirmity, that whatever good we can do, whatever ability we may have, we may be that in Him; that 'he that glorieth may glory in the Lord' " (1 Corinthians 1:31) from *On the Psalms 38.*

Warren Thomas Smith
The Interdenominational Theological Center
Atlanta, Georgia
Augustine's Day
August 28, 1979

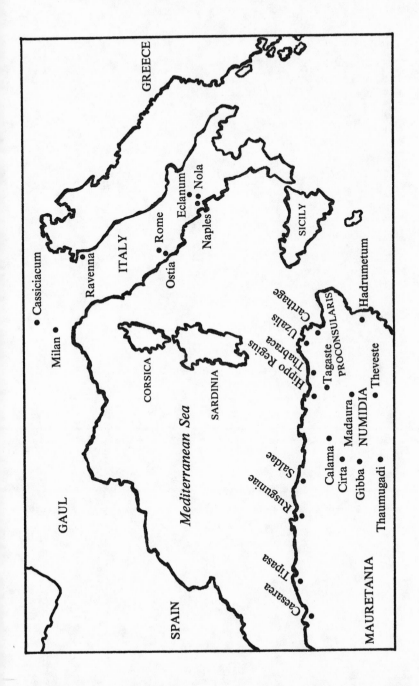

Contents

I

Augustine's World

Pax Romana

It was a tumultuous age—mid-fourth century A.D.—in which Augustine was born. For almost a thousand years Rome had flourished by the Tiber, a symbol of stable government, a solidity which prevailed in spite of Rome's engagement in almost continual conquest. No section of the Mediterranean had experienced the full force of Roman arms quite to the extent as Africa.

As long ago as 509 B.C. the sturdy Roman Republic, guided by a thoughtful, astute Senate and carefully watched by a patricio-plebeian aristocracy, felt the call of destiny. The Mediterranean must be patrolled and subdued—*mare nostrum* ("our sea") they called it—a Roman lake! Standing athwart Rome's ambition loomed ancient Carthage, symbol of Phoenician Africa, rich and proud.

Divide et impera was Rome's plan, and after conquest, partition her enemies she did. Conquering Africa, however, proved to be long and costly. In 395 B.C. she attacked Carthage and Tunis. The native African population, as expected, lacked unity and was thus less than effective. The result was that Rome began the gradual formation of her invaluable provinces in Africa. Never would Africans forget the long, devastating Punic Wars. The first bloody conflict lasted 264–241 B.C. as Hanno, Hasdrubal, and Hamilcar Barca out-maneuvered the Roman fleet and harried the Italian coast, only to face defeat at the Aegates Islands. It was an expensive victory. Rome lost 700 ships (manned by 140,000 sailors) compared to Carthage's forfeiture of 500 vessels. In 238 B.C., Sardinia and Corsicia were snatched from Carthage and shortly the war drums once more sounded. The Second Punic War, 218–216B.C., witnessed the Carthaginian forces led first by Hasdrubal, then by the magnificent Hannibal. Rome trembled when couriers brought word of the invading host of 26,000 Africans plus the celebrated elephant corps which had marched across Spain, Gaul, and over the Alps and into the Po valley. Rome was able to put immense armies into the field but Hannibal brilliantly defeated three of them in succession: at Trevia in 218, Trasimene the following year, and Canne in 216. In spite of these astounding victories, Hannibal failed to attack the city itself. Finally Scipio annihilated the Carthaginian forces, and six years later a war-weary Carthage was compelled to accept Rome's humiliating terms of surrender: payment of 200 talents in gold a year for fifty years, burning of all but ten of her war galleys, and the promise not to make war without Rome's permission. Scipio's greatest reward was his title *Africanus*.

Valiant Carthage made a final attempt to curb Rome's power in 149–146 B.C. with the Third Punic War, and was met by Cato's cry to the Senate, "Carthage must be destroyed." It came to pass in 146 B.C. as a proud African municipality was put to the torch, her buildings razed, her high-minded populace plundered, and the territory (that which we call Tunisia) annexed as the "Province of Africa."

Rome did not delay in making the conquered territory thoroughly Roman. Within twenty years Gracchus established 6,000 *coloni*—retired soldiers and sailors who, for the most part, became small landholders—in Numidia. King Jugurtha skillfully massacred the sons of Micipsa at Cirta, but Rome sought revenge, and he was defeated by Marius. Later there was Pompey's short-lived revolt in which he was aided by Juba, King of Numidia.[1] Under Julius Caesar, however, Rome was once more victorious at Thapsus. Numidia, now known as "Africa Nova," was added to the Province of Africa. There still remained the stubbornly independent Republic of Cirta.

It was the sagacious Julius Caesar who carefully and systematically Latinized Africa. From his time until the close of Tiberius' reign, A.D. 37, the vast Province of Africa extended from Cyrene to the River Ampsaga. The portion of the African coast from Cyrene to Thabraca was designated Proconsular Africa. To the west, Cirta and the interior region was governed by a Praetor and under him was the famed African Legion. Iol—later known as Caesarea—was ruled by King Bocchus;

Tingi (Tangiers) was under King Bogud. Later these areas were unified under King Juba II and his son Ptolemy. In A.D. 40 the Provinces of Mauretania Caesariensis and Mauretania Tingitana came into being. A third province, Mauretania Sitifensis, was created much later, in A.D. 260.

It was during Diocletian's brilliant reign that clear divisions were made in Africa. Mauretania Tingitana was transferred to the Diocese of Spain. The Diocese of Africa embraced *Tripolitania* (Cyrenaica to Lake Triton); *Byzacena* (Lake Triton to Horrea); *Africa Proper* (Horrea to Tabarka); *Numidia* (Tabarka to the River Ampsaga); *Mauretania Sitifensis* (River Ampsaga to Saldae); *Mauretania Caesariensis* (Saldae to the River Malva).[2] Generally, a Roman would have regarded as Africa that sprawling coastline starting at Cyrenaica, extending to Tripolitania and continuing to include Proconsular Africa and Numidia. Territory west of Numidia was known as Mauretania. Augustine's African years were spent almost exclusively in Numidia and Proconsular Africa. He spoke of having "seen the walls of Carthage, but not the walls of Alexandria."

At the time of Augustine's birth the Roman Empire had long passed its prime. It was still a vast colossus standing astride most of Europe, Asia Minor, extending through Syria and Palestine and including all of North Africa. It was a territory too large to administer—over two and one half million square miles. Attempting to govern sixty-six million inhabitants—to say nothing of teeming throngs of so called "barbarians" living at the borders—was virtually impossible. Solidarity had disappeared. Allegiance, clearly demonstrated in Africia, was to the Provinces, not to Rome itself. Many factors combined to create a governmental and social situation vastly complex and completely unwieldly.

The power of the Senate was virtually gone, and the army—or sections thereof—proclaimed emperors with abandon. It was a time of murder, massacres, coups d'état. In the year A.D. 307 alone there had been six emperors. Fatigue was clearly evident. The zestful, virile Roman spirit had long since waned. It was under Diocletian in A.D. 285 that the final, grand phase of empire was attempted, and the scheme endured through Constantine and his heirs. It was an autocratic regime; order was restored for the time being. To carry out a despotic rule, larger and larger armies were required. These were not the old Roman legions, but innumerable companies of non-Roman mercenaries—especially Germanic peoples—employed to defend a weak frontier. To pay for adequate protection immense sums were essential, taxes were constantly increased, and there was an ever growing demand for imported food. Fiscal policy—if there were a policy—at the beginning of the fourth century was in utter chaos.

Perhaps the most ruinous aspect of Roman life was loss of civic pride. "Romans no longer believed in the greatness of Rome." First-rate talent was employed for personal gain rather than in dedication to the common good. In the Provinces the same malediction prevailed; public office holders were usually out for personal gratification. "For when can that lust for power in arrogant hearts come to rest until, after passing from one office to another, it arrives at sovereignty?" asked Augustine.[3]

Nonetheless, Rome had done her work well. She had built beautiful cities adorned with hospitals, universities, libraries, public baths, and magnificent homes. Her aqueducts, harbors, and roads were superb. She had enriched the land—especially in Africa—by planting millions of trees. Her language and culture had been freely distributed. Above all, she had provided justice and a concept of law, and with it order and stability. In a word, Rome bequeathed civilization to millions upon millions. True, it was a Greco-Roman culture, but the majority of mankind benefited. Imperious Rome's faults were many; so were her virtues. Now it was all coming to expiration: soft glow of twilight for an empire which had served its purpose in history and was now fading away. An amazing paradox persisted. While multitudes saw the disintegration, they refused to accept it. Augustine's Africa, for the most part, went about daily living in naïve supposition that nothing was going to change, unaware of the fatal malaise. When the end came, the blow proved overwhelming.

Repercussion to Rome's demise was softened due to Constantine's having transferred the seat of empire from Italy to Constantinople in A.D. 330. For the West—and Africa was included—it was the conclusion of authentic Roman power. Emperors were consistently impotent —politically—and increasingly ineffective. It proved to be an altogether different story in the East. A magnificent Byzantine Empire was born, to flourish and endure for almost a thousand years. Constantinople became the "Second Rome." It took on its own distinct personality: Greek orientation, heavily influenced by Persia and Syria. The very fact of continuity in the East gave a faint sense of endurance in the West.

Life of the Church

Augustine's life spanned one of the most dynamic epochs in Christian history. The fourth century opened with Constantine's nominal acceptance of the Christian faith, A.D. 312, even though actual rite of baptism was reserved until the Emperor's deathbed. A new climate was experienced. No longer was a pagan emperor to be feared, distrusted as anti-Christ, an avenger and persecutor—save for the brief interlude of Julian the Apostate, the one who now wore the imperial purple assumed the role of champion of Christ, giving his personal dignity and tremendous prestige to the Christian cause.

This was the era in which monasticism experienced remarkable growth in Palestine, Syria, throughout Asia Minor, but especially in Egypt and Augustine's own North Africa. Anthony (250–356?), upon whom legend fixed an almost impossible longevity, encountered his tormenting demons in the desert. There followed Pachomius, with the establishment of the first Christian monastery at Tabennisi in southern Egypt. Simon Stylites spent thirty years atop his pillar near Antioch. It was Basil who set the pattern for Eastern monasticism; for the West, Benedict with his famous rule—but the latter was not to come until at least a century after Augustine. These were strategic years for the monastic ideal, now firmly established, and Augustine himself played no small part in drawing up standards for a cause which was destined to become a major facet of Christian lifestyle.

Church buildings assumed a prominent place in the thinking of local congregations. Free now to worship in public, Christians took understandable pride in the construction of houses of worship. Africa was especially noted for magnificent marble basilicas and baptistries as well as houses for priests and residences for orders of nuns. Exquisite mosaics adorned floors, walls, ceilings. These were not small edifices. Indeed, crowds of many hundreds could be accommodated. At times walled basilicas became fortresses. Augustine recalled Ambrose's situation in Milan, when imperial troops laid siege to the bishop and his congregation.

Of all achievements, the most brilliant was in theology itself, the "golden age" of patristics. Giants such as Irenaeus and Clement and Origen had paved the way. Africa had given the church Tertullian and Cyprian. Within Augustine's own life span Athanasius was standard-bearer, contending for the creed. Basil was born in 329, twenty-five years prior to Augustine. Within that range were born Gregory Nizianzan, Gregory of Nyssa, John Chrysostom, Ambrose, and Jerome.[4] A heady, exhilarating era it was. Theological controversy became habitual in the major councils, beginning with Nicaea in 325, Constantinople in 381, Ephesus in 431, Chalcedon in 451. Africa was the scene of numerous conclaves, and Augustine surged forward as a stellar figure. Debate and writing of papers became the order of the day and the "queen of the sciences" ruled in splendor—even if the exchange involved bickering and the tactics of a dog fight. Major doctrinal themes were being hammered out on an anvil of deep human experience. Heresies such as Arianism and Donatism, and counter forces, Manichaeism and the like, had to be dealt with.

The maturing church was finding and expressing herself. Scripture was in translation as Jerome brooded over manuscripts in his cell in Bethlehem. The role and function of bishop as teacher and defender of doctrine was coming into clear focus. Having come through the conflagration of persecution and having been bathed in the blood of the martyrs, the church—and especially the African Church—was equipping herself for mission. And no single individual assumed a more important posture of leadership in this mission than Augustine. "He that is born in the fire," runs an African poverb, "will not melt in the sun." The African Church—and Augustine—would have ample opportunity to prove it.

> You are sons of the Church, and have profited in the Church, and you who have not as yet profited in the Church will profit in the Church, and you who have already profited have no profit further in the Church.[5]

II

Home and Parents

Tagaste

The Sahara, the world's largest desert, spreads more than three thousand miles across Africa, from the Atlantic to the Red Sea. It is a thousand-mile-wide band of windswept, stony desert, interspersed with sere highlands and vast expanses of shifting sand. Its domain is awesome, powerful, reaching to Father Nile. Above the Sahara we find the Atlas Mountains, spreading from the southwestern section of modern Morocco, sweeping up to the ancient Pillars of Hercules and on to the northeastern tip of modern Tunesia. Some mountain peaks of the High Atlas tower above 13,000 feet. Within the area of the Atlas Mountains there is a moist, temperate Mediterranean climate, a territory of green vegetation and cool streams, yet one which knows the searing blasts of the sirocco. Here we find our story's locale.

Known today as Souk Ahras in Algeria, Tagaste was a city with more than three hundred years of history at the time Augustine was born. Located on the road between Hippo (the modern city of Bône) and Madaura (Mdaourouch), and half-way between Carthage (Tunis) and Cirta (Constantine),[1] it had once belonged to the province of ancient Numidia. In Augustine's day Tagaste was governed from Carthage. The town was some two hundred miles inland. "We who were born and brought up among Mediterranean peoples were able, even as children," he later wrote, "to imagine the sea, from seeing water in a small cup."[2]

Tagaste was on an elevation of two thousand feet. Boundless forests of olive trees had been planted throughout the area—oil was a major export. Augustine frequently referred to the olive presses. As a mature scholar he rejoiced for there was abundance of oil for midnight study. There were also pines and yew in profusion. The countryside was inviting: open spaces with cork trees provided plenty of pheasants, quail, thrush, and even wild boar. In remote sections the caracal, jackal, and Barbary sheep were found; the lordly lion roamed and Augustine later likened the Donatists to "roaring lions."[3] It was an ideal situation for a growing boy. It is not difficult to envision the elderly bishop in Hippo recalling his days as a lad, hiking through the countryside. "Why, then, as a boy could I cover more ground in hunting birds without getting tired than when, as a young man, I devoted myself to other studies."[4]

Farming was all important, and most of the population eked out the best living they could. Those who made money were the wealthy few, the *patroni* who owned huge estates and lived ostentatiously. Their splendid villas were replete with cypress groves and orchards. They had extensive vineyards and unending fields of grain—Africa was the granary of Rome. Fish ponds were well stocked and there were huge barns and stables. Multitudes of servants were of course required. Augustine vividly remembered these impressive holdings. He sadly recounted the situations "on large estates, grazing and tillage—the poor despoiled of their flocks in order to provide sacrifices at pagan festivals."[5]

Augustine's own home was modest. How well he remembered the farming: "They cultivate land,"[6] he mentioned in a long letter. He also knew "sowing is done in the fall, after the earth has been saturated with the showers of autumn." He was enchanted by the rustic folklore: "Leap year was considered by the superstitious a bad time to plant a vineyard."[7] He could recall gardening and the hard work of the farm. In years to come in northern Italy he wrote of beginning the day by spending "a very short while with the farm hands."[8] Did Augustine really enjoy the rigors of farming, or was it memory of childhood? Similarly, he recalled that strawberries and cherries were not to be found "until we had tasted them in Italy."[9]

Tagaste was Augustine's hometown, place of his birth, his childhood, and he kept these scenes before him: "The power of memory is great, . . . awe-inspiring in its profound and incalculable complexity."[10] Yes, he vividly kept in mind "Tagaste, my native town."[11]

Patricius

Patricius Herculus was probably a small man, quite dark, "swarthy and with quick black eyes."[12] His background was doubtless that of the Berbers[13] or Moors—most of the citizens of Tagaste were of Berber stock—the oldest race in North Africa. Before the time of Egypt's pharaohs these Berbers inhabited much of northwest Africa. The ancient Phoenicians had engaged them in trade. Berbers live today in isolated villages as farmers and shepherds in the High Atlas. They were people tending to be short of stature, of dark complexion, wide shoulders, narrow hips, of nervous personality and energetic temperament. If this is an accurate portrait of his father's people, would it not give a reliable clue to Augustine's appearance and personality? It is rather well established that Augustine was a small man physically.

Patricius was a pagan. He was a member of "the very honorable municipal council" a *decurion*, full citizen of the Roman Empire, entitled to wear the impressive toga. When the African, Septimius Severus, became emperor he conferred rights of citizenship on all freemen born in those African territories which had been organized into municipalities. Naturally this delighted many Africans who, like Patricius, took Latin names and frequently ordered the phrase "One who has achieved Roman citizenship" carved on their tombs. Augustine tells us that his father, "a modest citizen of Tagaste,"[4] did not have wealth. We know that he owned land which he supervised.

Africa dramatically illustrated the stratified, entangled civilization of the time. Administration was in the hands of Romans who stood at the top of society; their language was Latin. Next were the *coloni*. There would also be Greek and Jewish merchants who traveled throughout the empire. Add to these Phoenicians, Arabs, Kabyles, Touaregs, and, especially, the Berbers, all of whom would have been part of Tagaste, and in a measure, part of Patricius. He might well have combined that fighting spirit of the ancient Numidians and the shrewdness of the Phoenicians together with administrative expertise of the

Romans.[15] He would have needed all, for as a member of the curial class he was taxed severely and at the same time expected to maintain a social life commensurate with the minor civic aristocracy. In later years Augustine spoke of himself as "poor, and who is the son of poor parents."[16] It was certainly not an egalitarian world.

Patricius was forty-six when Augustine was born. Augustine gives only one or two direct references to "the father who begat me."[17] It must have been in the spirit of largess that Augustine overstated the case; "No one had anything but praise for my father."[18] How close was the relationship between father and son? We cannot say with certainty, but there is no doubt it was overshadowed by Monica. She was the great force in the family—assuredly in the son's eyes. In several situations Patricius is mentioned, but only in relation to his wife: "Though he was remarkably kind, he had a hot temper, but my mother knew better than to say or do anything to resist him when he was angry."[19] Other women in Tagaste "knew well enough how hot-tempered a husband my mother had to cope with." Let it be said to Patricius' credit, these same gossips "had never heard, or seen any marks to show, that Patricius had beaten his wife."

Patricius' marriage to Monica had been arranged, as custom demanded; "when she was old enough, they gave her in marriage to a man."[20] He dominated the household—outwardly. In all probability he played a far greater role in the formation of his illustrious son's personality than either history or the son will admit. They shared a great many traits, not the least of which was a piquant sensuality!

Monica

Few women in Christian history have been venerated as extensively and persistently as has the mother of Augustine, and the son is largely responsible. All that we know of her we learn from him. Ten years elapsed between her death and the writing of the *Confessions*. Augustine's memory was immeasurably influenced by passing of time, for time can soften and beautify—especially when there has been fulfillment of matriarchal designs.

Monica was born into a Christian home with parents of—supposedly—godly, faithful backgrounds. Her name is Berber, possibly derived from the Libyan goddess Mon [Monday] worshipped in the nearby town of Thibilis.[21] She was "brought up in modesty and temperance."[22] It was a militant puritanism, and the sole flaw in her childhood seems to have been fondness for wine. It definitely makes a good story, which is possibly the reason Augustine tells it. Monica was reared by a faithful slave, "an aged servant, who had carried my grandfather." At meals water was never served the children "for fear they might develop bad habits." Alas, Monica's single household responsibility was to draw table wine from the cast and "she would sip a few drops" in the process. Daily an increased number was consumed until one servant in a fit of anger "called my mother a drunkard." It struck home!

Monica set out to be both model wife and exemplar Christian. She would convert Patricius. Admittedly he "was unfaithful to her, but her patience was so great that his infidelity never became a cause of quarrelling." When his temper raged "my mother knew better than to say or do anything to resist him when he was angry." Other townswomen marveled and then complained "of the behavior of their menfolk." Monica advised them to hold their tongues, refrain from resisting, and never defy their masters—as so stipulated in the marriage contract. Accordingly she escaped customary beatings.

Monica faced a problem: a mother-in-law who was "at first prejudiced against her"[23] thanks to the gossip of slaves. This "tale-bearing of malicious servants" came to a halt when Patricius—theoretical head of the ménage—had the offending ones whipped. It was Monica's long-suffering and amiability that eventually prevailed "and the two women lived together in wonderful harmony and mutual good will." As Augustine writes—in retrospect—Monica becomes sign and symbol of the faithful Christian who, with infinite forbearance, never gives up, never fails to be loving, for "in the end she won her husband . . . as a convert in the very last days of his life." She is almost too good to be true. Fortunately, Augustine weaves Monica's story into his own experience in such a natural, almost guileless narrative that the reader sees a real woman — in spite of her son's attempt to explain away her humanity. Monica was a female with resolve, an African lioness who fought for her cub. Beneath an exterior of naïveté there existed a crafty politician who knew how to play people and causes one against the other. Augustine had a remarkable mother.

In Augustine's home we have a vivid demonstration of the clash between Christian and pagan cultures. His parents embodied piety versus sensuality. Perhaps this tension would be forever a part of Augustine's makeup.

III

Childhood and Youth
A.D. 354–370

Patricius would have been forty-one and Monica eighteen at the time of their marriage. Their first-born was a son, Navigius. A daughter came next; her name is not recorded by Augustine, but tradition designates her as Perpetua.[1] She later married, was widowed, and in after years became a nun in Hippo. Another daughter may have been born to Monica and Patricius.

On Sunday, November 13, 354, after five years of wedded life, Monica and Patricius became parents of a second son; they named him Aurelius Augustinus. "Perhaps you too may laugh at me, . . . Lord, . . . I do not know where I came from."[2] Nor did the world care, certainly not Liberius who sat in Peter's Chair in Rome, nor Constantius II, Emperor at Ravenna.

Augustine interminably dwells on his own infancy, and infancy in general, obviously fascinated by the whole prospect of birth and growth; he loved babies. "All I knew was how to suck, and how to lie still when my body sensed comfort or cry when it felt pain." He continued in a more theological vein, "Who can recall to me the sins I have committed as a baby?" Or again, "I have myself seen jealousy in a baby and know what it means." Was it an obsession, this unwavering interest in prenatal existence, mystery of birth, infancy? "You, O Lord my God, gave me my life and my body when I was born. You gave my body its five senses; . . . limbs . . . proper proportions; . . . all the instincts necessary for the welfare and safety of a living creature." Very thoughtfully he draws his conclusion about the essence of life, "I do

not like to think of that period as part of the same life I now lead, . . .
in this sense, it is no different from the time I spent in my mother's
womb . . . when was I . . . ever innocent?"[3] It must not escape notice
that in later years Augustine the theologian was of this opinion:

> In fact is there anyone who, faced with the choice between
> death and a second childhood, would not shrink in dread from
> the latter prospect and elect to die? Infancy, indeed, starts this
> life, not with smiles but with tears; and this is, in a way, an
> unconscious prophecy of the troubles on which it is entering.[4]

Augustine was not baptized in infancy, but the rite of the Cross on
the forehead and the cleansing touch of salt upon the lips was observed,
"sign of the Cross . . . seasoned with God's salt."[5] Once a "disorder
of the stomach" made him so ill it was feared he would die. "I appealed to the piety of my own mother . . . to give me the baptism of
Christ. . . . Had I not quickly recovered, she would have hastened to
see that I was admitted to the sacraments of salvation." Reason for delay was patent to a good Catholic. "Washing in the waters of baptism"
was postponed lest "I should defile myself again with sin and . . . the
guilt of pollution would be greater and more dangerous."

It all transpired so quickly. "The next stage of my life, . . . was
boyhood. Or would it be truer to say that boyhood overtook me." Long
before he could use words properly, Augustine recalls a "universal language . . . expressions of the face and eyes, gestures and tone of
voice." As he "took a further step into the stormy life of human society" he encountered language—and never ceased to be enthralled by it.
Latin was his favorite. He probably knew almost nothing in old Berber
—spoken by peoples of the Numidian plains. He doubtless had but
scant knowledge of Punic, nonetheless he always held it in high regard.
In writing to Maximus in 390 he put it bluntly, "I do not think you
could have forgotten that [you are] an African writing to Africans,
since we are both settled in Africa, would scarcely think that Punic
names were objectionable."[6]

Augustine's schoolboy days are tragic, "a period of suffering and
humiliation."[7] He was flogged. He was quite young and did not understand particular instruction or direction given by the inept teacher, so
was needlessly and sadistically chastised. He prayed, "I begged you

not to let me be beaten at school." Games offered mild relief, but the small boys were even "punished for them" and trounced by hypocritical adults who enjoyed the identical sports. Obviously these cruel school days were never put out of mind; the haunting specter remained with the mature bishop.

Augustine's Latin was a joy—once the accursed grammar was over, "I loved Latin, not the elementary lessons." Greek became another matter, "I cannot fully understand why the Greek language, . . . was so distasteful to me." In years to come Augustine was to have this omission flaunted in his face; no less a figure than Jerome caustically reminded Augustine of this glaring deficiency.

As a lad Augustine memorized the "wanderings of a hero named Aeneas" and wept at "the fate of Dido" queen of Carthage. He doted on "empty romances," the wooden horse, the burning of Troy, the ghost of Creusa. He was forced to study Homer and disliked him. Augustine may have detested Greek grammar but he admitted the tales were fascinating. Ah, Latin. Vergil he idolized. It is nothing less than a wonder he enjoyed school at all; dull, routine methods were customary. Little boys were required to sit on rough mats, repeating in monotonous singsong chant the words of the *primus magister* (first teacher): a melancholy ordeal indeed.

Respite came through those delightful immature experiences after school when there was reenactment of mature African dramas: Dido's suicide; the Trojan hero's perpetual wandering; hours lived in a brilliant world of fantasy. Then, returning to a dull, unimaginative mentor, "if I put . . . the question whether it is true, . . . that Aeneas once came to Carthage, the less learned will plead ignorance and the better informed will admit that it is not true."[8]

In fairness to the brutal educational system, it had a goal, even for students at this early stage: perfection in the use of words. "I should have wished you to give me such skill in writing and such power in framing words,"[9] prayed Augustine. Painful though it was, through relentless drill, Augustine captured the art of expression, he knew "wisdom and folly can be clothed alike in plain words or the finest flowers of speech."[10] He learned to express "feelings of sorrow and anger appropriate to the majesty of the character . . . impersonated." Later he wondered "Why did my recitation win more praise than those of the many other boys?" He called it "smoke without fire" but in reality it was the dawn of finely honed oratorical skill.

Days at Tagaste would have been spent in bright sunlight, African brilliance. Light would forever have special meaning for Augustine, "light, the queen of colours . . . wins so firm a hold on me that, if I am suddenly deprived of it, I long to have it back."[11] It was inevitable that glorious sunlight would be reminder of the "true Light" so often mentioned in later writings. He did not like sodden winter months of rain and fog, dampness and cold. He was African, his experience was life in warm sunlight; happiness was Tagaste in the sun. "Take an African," he would later say to his people at Hippo, "put him in a place cool and green, and he won't stay there. He will feel he must go away and come back to his blazing desert."

Augustine noted the contrast of brightness, "I said that the beauty of the day is enhanced by comparison with night, as the color white is more lovely by contrast with black."[12]

At Madaura

At fifteen Augustine was sent to neighboring Madaura—some thirty miles away—for continued schooling. He had proved to be a capable, if not superior, student, and funds were made available. It was in this new town that he found himself surrounded by blatant paganism, far in excess of anything in Tagaste. Not only were there statues of the gods everywhere, but in Madaura were more inscriptions than perhaps in any other city in Africa. It was also here that the renowned second century orator and writer, Apuleius, was celebrated. Much later, in decrying the obscenities used by poets describing gods, men and demons, Augustine observed, "These ideas can be found in many writers; but the Platonist Apuleius of Madaura has devoted a whole book to the subject, under the title, *The God of Socrates*."[13] Augustine dismissed Apuleius as a dealer in magic, and his work as a fabrication which ought to have been called *The Demon of Socrates*. Apuleius' most noted work, *The Golden Ass*, was usually regarded as a classic. "Apuleius, who as an African is better known to us Africans," noted Augustine in a later writing, "was not able, for all his magic arts, to achieve any judicial power in the state."[14]

School at Madaura would have been in a large hut, curtained from the street. Augustine's schoolmaster would have worn distinctive dress and received a salary from local authorities as well as fees from the students. Augustine speaks of "how I squandered the brains" God had freely bestowed "on foolish delusions."[15] What were the texts used here, as well as in Tagaste? "This traditional education taught me that Jupiter punishes the wicked with his thunderbolts and yet commits adultery himself." Lewd, pornographic illustrations were constantly used by that "Idol of Africa"—Carthage-born Terence. He "brings on to the stage a dissolute youth who excuses his own fornication by pointing to the example of Jupiter."[16] "Filth" said Augustine, and he "gladly took a sinful pleasure in [it]. And for this very reason I was called a promising boy." He won more praise than any other student for his recitations, but he later wished there had been other subjects on which he might have "sharpened my wits and my tongue." Yes, he had become astute. He knew the appropriate terms for sorrow, anger, for he had learned to model himself after "men who revelled in the applause they earned for the fine flow of well-ordered and nicely balanced phrases." He was getting along in the world of elocution; he was likewise establishing a master rhetorician's expertise which was to be his for his lifetime.

Adolescence

Suddenly, "my studies were interrupted. I had already begun to go to the near-by town of Madaura to study literature and the art of public speaking."[17] Patricius needed time to collect sufficient funds for additional education at Carthage. Veritably, "despite his slender resources," somehow he would provide money. Many wealthy fathers in Tagaste did far less for their offspring. Patricius was ambitious for his son, but a wistful Augustine sadly observed that his father's one concern was "that I should have a fertile tongue." No thought was given to spiritual or moral development.

It was a miserable year, 370. Augustine, now sixteen, was experiencing all the pangs of adolescence, and no one offered real counsel, "certainly not my father." Patricius, on the other hand, was jubilant when "one day at the public baths he saw the signs of active virility coming to life in me." Now grandchildren became a real possibility. (We wonder why a similar question was not raised regarding the two older children. But they are out of the picture—Augustine is telling the story.) Augustine almost resented Patricius' pride in physical growth and academic achievement. Had the father no interest in a deep-seated, personal father-son relationship? For the moment "he was happy to tell my mother" their son was becoming a man.

By this time Patricius had become a catechumen. He was moving in the direction of a life of faith and would in due time become a Catholic. Monica was responsible, to be sure. Now a new concern came to her, that the youthful Augustine avoid a "crooked path." She advised, most earnestly, that he not commit fornication and that "above all" he not seduce another man's wife. Seduction of a maiden, or sexual relations with a trollop apparently constituted a lesser sin—a double standard accepted in the fourth century quite as glibly as today.

To what extent was young Augustine the sinner? "If I had not sinned enough to rival other sinners, I used to pretend." Is the Bishop of Hippo reading back into his teen years a moral condition that does not really belong? Was he so utterly lost in sensuality? The story of the pear tree almost teases a smile:

> There was a pear-tree near our vineyard, loaded with fruit that was attractive neither to look at nor to taste. Late one night a band of ruffians, myself included, went off to shake down the fruit and carry it away, for we had continued our games out of doors until well after dark, as was our pernicious habit. We took away an enormous quantity of pears, not to eat them ourselves, but simply to throw them to the pigs.[18]

He concluded his story, "The evil in me was foul, but I loved it." The notion "it was robbery" haunted his soul, "still alive in my memory." "It was the sin that gave it flavour." Hence the shocking import of the whole episode: while it may appear but a bagatelle, hardly worth mentioning, to Augustine it was willful sinning. Africans tended to think a boy innocent until he reached puberty, "as if the only sins," said Augustine, "you could commit were those in which you use your genitals."[19]

IV

Student Days
A.D. 371–375

Rome had ruled Carthage for five and a half centuries by the time Augustine arrived in 371 as a university student. "I found myself in the midst of a hissing cauldron of lust."[1] He was seventeen. He had come to "Carthage of Venus" in order to put the finishing touches on his preparation as an orator. He had now mastered the Latin classics: Cicero, Sallust, Terence, and especially Vergil—"outstandingly the best" —which he had loved since the first reading as a child.[2] His academic foundation was somewhat limited, with no broad introduction to history or philosophy and almost no science (fields he would later master quite on his own), but he was becoming an artist in both the written and spoken phrase, one who weighed "the precise sense"[3] of every word. And few there are in Western culture who could ever claim to be his equal in the use of words. He was not restricting his field of operation; "Besides these pursuits I was also studying for the law." He felt "ambition was held to be honourable and I determined to succeed in it."

Scholarly pursuits were not Augustine's great disquietude; the temptation to join other indolent men in pursuing pleasure was the issue. During these hapless years he took a concubine, a nameless girl who was to share his life for the next fifteen years. "I had not yet fallen in love, but I was in love with the idea of it, and this feeling that something was missing made me despise myself for not being more anxious to satisfy the need."[4] Where did he find her? Was she a prostitute? He does not say. Yet, with transparent honesty, he recounts his emotional war, seeking "some object for my love" yet not willing to follow "the

safe path" Monica suggested. It was a desire "to have ambitions of
cutting a fine figure in the world." He blandly admitted it was "a snare
of my own choosing," this love which gripped so persistently:

> My love was returned and finally shackled me in the bonds of
> its consummation. In the midst of my joy I was caught up in the
> coils of trouble, for I was lashed with the cruel, fiery rods of
> jealousy and suspicion, fear, anger, and quarrels.[5]

Carthage boasted an enormous theatre where salacious produc-
tions proved a tantalizing delight "because the plays reflected my
own unhappy plight." It was sensual involvement, emotional participation, "tinder to my fire" wherein the youthful, amorous swain
"used to share the joy of stage lovers and their sinful pleasures."
Admittedly he wholeheartedly enjoyed "fables and fictions" yet at
the same time considered it depravity, "the bottom-most depths of
scepticism," but "I loved my own way . . . a truant's freedom."
We must remember that Augustine was living within a milieu which
encouraged the life of a libertine. He would have been an oddity had
he refrained from entanglement. It was Carthaginian paganism, and
he was manacled to it.

Augustine had joined a gang known as the Wreckers, "a title of ferocious devilry which the fashionable set chose for themselves."[6]
While he may have had little to do with their malicious outbursts he
"lived among them, feeling a perverse sense of shame because I was
not like them." He gleefully watched them "set upon some timid newcomer, gratuitously affronting his sense of decency for their own
amusement."[7]

At this time Augustine was not a professing Catholic. At best he
regarded himself a student of law and "the art of eloquence." Moral
standards—as Monica knew them—had been left with her. He was a
romantic pagan having a rousing good time. In retrospect, Augustine
abhorred the pricks of sin whereby "the skin becomes inflamed. It
swells and festers with hideous pus." But this was reminiscence. Exis-
tentially, he was a youth "at that impressionable age" fired by ambition "to be a good speaker," caught up in a sensual, permissive
society.

Cicero

In the midst of his "prescribed course of study" Augustine chanced upon Cicero's *Hortensius*. "It altered my outlook on life,"[8] and this now irreclaimable treasure, a volume describing the glory of philosophy, brought "new hopes and aspirations." Unexpectedly his heart pounded with the romance of learning, "a bewildering passion for the wisdom of eternal truth." This moment in no small degree represents a "climb out of the depths"; there was now at least a quest for learning. Not so much style as content "won me over" and all the while Augustine was supposed to be polishing his oratorical talent, "I did not use the book as a whetstone to sharpen my tongue." And the whole purpose in the little money coming from Monica "was supposed to be spent in putting an edge on my tongue." It was wanton deception. This financial assistance, modest as it may have been, was fulfillment of Patricius' dream, "I was now in my nineteenth year," said Augustine. With sober reflection he recalled his mother, "she supported me," then, almost as an afterthought he adds, "because my father had died two years before." How casually Patricius is dismissed—in utter contrast to the time devoted to Monica.

Hortensius wrought an intellectual transformation. Augustine fell in love with the concept of Wisdom. With sophomoric delight he tells of "these so-called philosophers who lived in Cicero's time and before are noted in the book. He shows them up in their true colours." He readily, and joyfully, admits that through Cicero he was drawn to God. At the outset it was a pagan desire "to love wisdom itself . . . pursue it, hold it, and embrace it firmly." And it was wisdom which "made no mention of the name of Christ."[9] It was heathenism—lofty to be sure, which "ignored the saving name of Christ." Nonetheless, the first step had been taken in a lifelong quest for philosophical understanding. As long as he lived, Augustine remained a philosopher, or at least he retained a philosopher's love for wisdom.

A natural prompting, a second step, followed, "So I made up my mind to examine the holy Scriptures and see what kind of books they were." Lo, a grave disappointment: "To me they seemed quite unworthy of comparison with the stately prose of Cicero." Crudities of the

60791

Old Testament proved most offensive, "whether men could be called just if they had more than one wife at the same time, or killed other men, or sacrificed living animals." Augustine raised multitudes of queries regarding "true underlying justice" and its application to "Abraham and Isaac, Jacob, Moses, David." These so-called human predicaments seemed almost bogus. Later Augustine would view Scripture as a missive from God, but upon first reading—his introduction to the Bible—it was anything but auspicious. He regarded himself too proud to bow his head to enter its mysteries: "what may be done, or must be done, in one room is forbidden and punished in another. This does not mean that justice is erratic or variable, but that the times over which it presides are not always the same, for it is the nature of time to change. . . . I knew nothing of this at that time. I was quite unconscious of it, quite blind to it, although it stared me in the face."[10]

Augustine's intellectual battle becomes all the more pointed when we realize that the fourth century African Church (at least when compared to twentieth century views) held to a very conservative interpretation of Scripture. The Bible was sacred, to be defended. While this view was not limited to Africa, in Africa it was often carried to extremes. Scripture, therefore, became part of the total questing life of a young student. Like philosophy, Scripture burst upon Augustine like brilliant African sunshine, but the flood of brightness did not come until he had opened the louvered window. The ventilating would eventually come, but at the moment he was fumbling with the latch.

Many years later, Augustine the bishop thoughtfully observed, "We need not despair of any man, so long as he lives."[11] Was he thinking of his own life? We do not know; but his observation is apropos. He knew what slow, anguished searching can mean.

> As spiritual grace descending upon us starts from wisdom and ends at fear, we are in ascending, struggling from the lowest to the highest, must start from fear and end at wisdom. "The fear of the Lord is the beginning of wisdom."[12]

Manichaeism

It was while Augustine was experiencing new-found liberation in philosophy and keen letdown in Holy Writ that he stumbled upon Manichaeism: the sect of Mani, a Persian crucified in A.D. 276. The zeal of the devotees, the "Elect," was amazing. Inordinately secretive, they surrounded themselves with all the trappings of oriental mystery. Theirs was the only true revelation; they were called to replace all other faiths, especially the Catholic. Their first representatives arrived in Carthage as early as A.D. 297[13] where they labored assiduously. It was the new experience, latest vogue, naturally creating quite a stir among so-called intellectuals. Augustine was the perfect target, so "I fell in with a set of sensualists, men with glib tongues who ranted and raved." For nine years he remained a Hearer, and "the dishes they set before me were still loaded with dazzling fantasies. . . . I gulped down this food."[14]

Passionately evangelistic and far more rigid than the Gnostics, the Manichees made rapid and wide growth, spreading out from the homeland of Babylonia, making special gains in the Far East where multitudes of Chinese responded.

Manichaeism offered the type of pseudo-philosophical faith that would appeal to young Augustine the pseudo-intellectual. It was based on the concept of eternal dualism: Good vs. Evil. Princes of Light—God and the Divine Messenger of Light—were forever contending with Demons of Darkness, seen especially in the Devil, whose Messengers were the Archons. Parts of the divine substance, Light, had been purloined by the Demons who, in turn, gave it to the Prince of Darkness. Using this filched treasure, the grim Prince created the world. All matter therefore is under his control, hence, *evil.* All flesh is under the domain of the Devil; man is his prime captive. Man does hold within himself a portion of Light, consequently his lot becomes an everlasting struggle to free himself from matter and darkness. There have been a great company of Messengers: Buddha, Zoroaster, Jesus, and, quite naturally, now Mani.

Manichees dwelt continually on the malefic nature of flesh. It was a motif in everything they said: all that is carnal is of darkness. God, totally good and absolutely innocent, can have no relationship with wickedness. It followed, naturally, since flesh is sinful God and flesh are never one.

What a paradox for Augustine, and what unbearable tension in his own sex life. As he slept with his woman his conscience may have recalled Monica's admonitions about Catholic continence. Now this

Manichaean prohibition on baneful, animalistic passion was "dinned in my ears over and over again!"[15] Is the sex act in itself evil? Mani would have thundered "Yes!" Ah, but Mani also provided a curious way out. It was not the *real* Augustine who was sinning, but the *evil* within. He might dissociate these carnal, lustful exploits from his soul, which was his authentic being. But these were fraudulent hopes. "Habits of any kind are so strong in their possession of the minds of men that, even in the case of those that are evil (and these usually come from the dominant passions)," Augustine wrote years afterwards, "we can more quickly condemn and detest them than we can abandon or change them." He continues:

> Do you think that there has been little regard for men, in that not only many learned men maintain in argument but also a multitude of unlearned men and women among them and such different classes of people both believe and assert that one should worship as God nothing earthly, nothing fiery, nothing which can touch the bodily senses, but that He can be reached only by the intellect? And what about the fact that self-restraint even leads to a very slim diet of bread and water? . . . that chastity is carried even to a rejection of marriage and a family?[16]

Manichaeism rendered one service to Augustine. The Old Testament could be cast aside blithefully. What a comfort to have Old Testament myths rejected, an immediate and gratifying solution. These Manichees were "exceedingly well-spoken and fashionable," expert in debate:

> And so they did to us what deceitful bird-catchers are wont to do, who fix lime-smeared branches near water to deceive thirsty birds. These men cover over and conceal in any way they can the other surrounding waters or even ward off the birds by formidable devices, so that they fall into snares, not through choice, but out of pure need.[17]

(Catching birds by smearing lime on branches was practiced by the Egyptians 1,500 years before the time of Christ.)

Good was always passive. Manichees spoke of the "Suffering Jesus" just as they spurned a stern Jehovah. Never—possibly because they were too astute to do so—did the Elect pose the question as to how

God, as source of tender generosity (grace) could also be the source of "punishment, vengeance and suffering" (judgement).[18]

Manichees assailed the Catholic position, frequently demolishing the arguments of the sanctimonious, the ill-informed. Through reason they would lead men to all truth. Augustine found himself in a delightful element. Catholics were, at best, sub-Christian or "semi-Christian."[19] The design of the Manichees was to infiltrate the church, and Augustine became their tool. He was emotionally, psychologically prepared for their gospel—now he could divest himself of the terrible father-figure of the Old Testament. The new Wisdom was his, and he had a Catholic background. He was zealous for the attack:

> I always used to win more arguments than was good for me, debating with unskilled Christians who had tried to stand up for their faith in argument. With this quick succession of triumphs the hot-headedness of a young man soon hardened into pigheadedness. As for this teachnique of argument, because I had set out on it after I had become a "Hearer" (among the Manichees), whatever I picked up by my own wits or by reading, I willingly ascribed to the effects of their teaching. And so, from their preaching, I gained an enthusiasm for religious controversy, and from this, I daily grew to love the Manichees more and more. So it came about that, to a surprising extent, I came to approve of whatever they said—not because I knew any better, but because I wanted it to be true.[20]

What rare sport it was, employing his forensic skill against some pious Catholic nincompoop. Words had become his stock in trade, and there was satisfaction in watching the discomfiture of an unnerved competitor. Did he have these scenes in mind when he later said, "Do we not carry our destruction about with us in this flesh? Are not we more brittle than if we were made of glass? Yet even though glass is brittle it lasts a long time if looked after; and you find cups which had belonged to grandfathers and great-grandfathers out of which their grandchildren and great-grandchildren are drinking. . . . But we men, brittle as we are, go about subject to such great accidents, that, even if the immediate mischance does not strike us, we cannot live for very long."[21]

It was a great life for a young inquirer, now quite full of himself. In retrospect, Augustine would look back on those years and call them sinful. And where does sin originate? He said it was in human pride wherein wicked humans "corrupt and pervert their own nature" which God had fashioned and shaped. Or people become "inflamed with passion" to make unnatural use of God's gifts. In short, when mere human beings attempt to be God, or assume God's power, that is sin.

Family

Augustine had his faithful common-law wife: "In those days I lived with a woman, not my lawful wedded wife but a mistress whom I chose for no special reason but that my restless passions had alighted on her."[22] If he had found her in a brothel, his feeling for her had moved to deep love, he wistfully continues:

> But she was the only one and I was faithful to her. Living with her I found out by my own experience the difference between the restraint of the marriage alliance, contracted for the purpose of having children, and a bargain struck for lust, in which the birth of children is begrudged, though if they come, we cannot help but love them.

Was she a Christian, at least in later years?[23] There is no question that it was genuine love. Perhaps there was scant intellectual content to the relationship—she was very likely poor and uneducated. Traditionalists have gone to absurd length to point out there was no tie of deep personal understanding.[24] Augustine's own words refute such notions. He loved her.

Augustine's situation was commonplace at that time in Africa, indeed, in all sections of the empire. He was a young student, a long way from establishing himself in his chosen profession, and one hardly claiming to be a Catholic. Few if any eyebrows would have been raised, and only a very strict moralist—Monica is a good example—would have regarded it a wanton arrangement, a liaison. Roman culture regarded this contrivance as handy, natural, and a practical answer to human sexuality without the inconvenience of formal marriage contracts.

Was a theologian-bishop thinking of his own past as, in Hippo, he penned these words?

The question is also usually asked whether this case ought to be called a marriage: when a man and a woman (he not being the husband nor she the wife of another) because of incontinence have intercourse not for the purpose of procreating children but only for the sake of intercourse itself, with this pledge between them, that he will not perform this act with another woman, nor she with another man. Yet perhaps not without reason can this be called wedlock, if this has been agreed upon between them even until the death of one of them and if, although they do not have intercourse for the purpose of having children, they do not avoid it, so that they do not refuse to have children nor act in any evil way so that they will not be born. But, if both or either one of these conditions is lacking, I do not see how we can call this a marriage.[25]

Augustine's subsequent view toward women—his written word, at least—became wholly Platonic, "As far as women are concerned, make me such a one as you wish; bestow upon her all sorts of gifts; there is nothing that I will avoid more than her company; for I feel that nothing is more capable of weakening the spirit of a man than the caresses of a woman." As far as he was affected personally, "I believe that I was rightly and justly concerned about the liberty of my soul, when I imposed upon myself the law of never desiring, seeking, nor marrying a woman."[26] Veritably, but was she totally forgotten—ever?

When Augustine was either eighteen or nineteen—A.D. 373 possibly—he became a father and named his son Adeodatus—Gift of God. Law at that time permitted Augustine, if he desired, to refuse any provision for the baby. Infanticide was very common. Mother and child could have been turned out any time. Not so. There developed a relationship between brilliant father and equally luminous (if we are to believe Augustine) son which is nothing less than beautiful. Augustine loved Adeodatus. The boy filled a niche in his father's life. It is sad, indeed, that Augustine insists upon referring to "my natural son born of my sin,"[27] but a penitent is writing, recollecting his wanton youthfulness. Regrettably the child born in those days is forever to bear the stigma of illegitimacy.

Adeodatus was born within the first years of Augustine's cohabitation with the mistress; the union was to continue for some twelve or more years. As both partners were quite young and, we assume, healthy, why were no other children born? Is it possible that Manichaean influence—and it came at just this time—was so strong that Augustine abstained from sexual relations? Was the sex act repressed, only to find expression in tormenting frustration and fantasy?

Teacher of Rhetoric

A Year in Tagaste A.D. 375

Augustine returned from Carthage to teach in his home town. A strange homecoming it was. He brought his concubine and Adeodatus, and his Manichaeism. It was the latter which proved too much for Monica. "Lately she had refused [to let Augustine live in her home] . . . because she loathed and shunned the blasphemy of my false beliefs."[1] Return to one's birthplace can pose problems aplenty; Augustine faced them all. His mother refused to accept his family, the woman at least, and this created heartbreaking strain in two directions. Monica always held a chief place in her son's affections. However untenable the family situation, it was Manichaeism which brought consternation. Augustine, in the fresh, glorious effervescence of the neophyte, was busy winning friends to his new, arcane faith. To Monica this was madness. Her hope, dream, and especially her prayer had been to win her husband—she won—and her son—she was losing—to the Catholic faith.

Monica continued to weep, adjure, and have far-fetched dreams:

> She dreamed that she was standing on a wooden rule, and coming towards her in a halo of splendour she saw a young man who smiled at her in joy, although she herself was sad and quite consumed with grief. He asked her the reason for her sorrow and her daily tears, not because he did not know, but because he had something to tell her. . . . When she replied that her tears were for the soul I had lost, he told her to take heart for, if she looked carefully, she would see that where she was, there also was I. And when she looked, she saw me standing beside her on the same rule.[2]

She made repeated visits to the priests. "Leave him alone," one bishop advised, "Just pray to God for him." With empathy the wise man added that he too, in his youth, had been misguided by the same Manichees. "From his own reading he will discover his mistakes and the depth of his profanity." Sage advice is frequently inadequate; Monica hung on, weeping, insisting the bishop make a personal visit to the wayward son. The good prelate at last became impatient, "Leave me and go in peace. It cannot be that the son of these tears should be lost." It might have been little more than a pious phrase to the bishop, anything to terminate an embarrassing scene; to Monica, who recounted the story, it was "a message from heaven."[3]

We must fill in many gaps during these months of emotional stress as Augustine attempted to make the best of it. "During these years I was a teacher of the art of public speaking." Money was not easy to come by; students posed ceaseless problems. He was teaching them trade secrets, "the tricks of pleading" and by so doing he was "merely abetting . . . their schemes of duplicity."[4] Completely guileless himself, he discovered the deceitfulness of others. On one occasion he entered a contest in "dramatic verse" whereupon a sorcerer offered, for a price, to "make certain" that he won. The offer was rejected on the spot, "I loathed and detested these foul rites and told him that even if the prize were a crown of gold that would last forever, I would not let even a fly be killed to win it. For he would have slaughtered living animals in his ritual."[5] By contrast, to Augustine, the "rites" of the Manichees appeared exceedingly attractive.

Here was Augustine: torn on the rack of personal and family conflicts, theological questionings and acute sense of moral guilt. Withal, to make the predicament more critical, veracity continued to be his marked characteristic. He may have been a sinner but he was not a liar.

Sweetness of Friendship

Throughout his life, Augustine found one of his cardinal outlets to be through friends and fellow believers. He gathered a small, select group about him in Tagaste; it became a life pattern. He had an African gregariousness. He was never an Anthony and he could not tolerate a hermit's life in an Egyptian desert. Though he enjoyed solitude—for prayer and study—he required fellowship. He painted his own portrait in living colors, "I hated to be wrong, had a vigorous memory, was well trained in speech, delighted in friendship, shunned pain, meanness and ignorance."[6]

Just what was Augustine doing? He and his associates were claiming to be the authentic Church of the Gentiles in Africa,[7] expressing a new thought—Wisdom—and with the condescending air of those lately come from Carthage to share with the provincial folk of Tagaste. It was a sophisticated, avant-garde cluster, snobbish in the extreme: "I was led astray myself and led others astray in my turn. We were alike deceivers. . . . In public we were cocksure, in private superstitious, and everywhere void and empty."[8] Who, then, were these compatriots? They are part of Augustine's life and personality. He depended upon them, not so much for counsel as for physical presence. It became an absolute necessity to have friends around him. To be cut off from people was intolerable.

Alypius

A member of the Tagaste band was one "greatly attached to me because he thought that I was a good and learned man, and I was fond of him because, although he was still young, it was quite clear that he had much natural disposition to goodness."[9] Alypius was probably the best friend Augustine ever had. He "came from my own town and his people were one of the leading families." Once in Carthage, Alypius had simply wandered into Augustine's class "and after greeting me politely sat down and listened attentively." In no time he came under Augustine's spell. How Augustine delighted in giving personal vignettes, as in Alypius' problem with Roman games, "this insane sport." Once in Rome he was taken to the arena much against his will and he even "shut his eyes tightly" insisting he would not even look. The roar of the crowd caused him to open his eyes, and in horror "he saw the blood . . . he fixed his eyes upon the scene and drank in all its frenzy . . . he revelled in the wickedness of the fighting and was drunk with the fascination of bloodshed." Another episode involved a thief and a hatchet; in attempting to apprehend the filcher, Alypius picked up the weapon which had been discarded. Alas, innocent soul that he was, he was seized—still holding the hatchet—and then handed "over to the magistrates."[10] These enjoyable experiences indicate a deep relationship. One is not apt to write trivia regarding a casual acquaintance.

Alypius "became a pupil of mine" and in due time was likewise "involved in my superstitious beliefs. He particularly admired the Manichees for their ostensible continence." Augustine goes to some length to delve into the most personal of relationships: "It was Alypius who prevented me from marrying, because he insisted that if I did so, we could not possibly live together in uninterrupted leisure," for "even as a grown man he was quite remarkably self-controlled in matters of sex. In early adolescence he had had the experience of sexual intercourse, but it had not become habitual. In fact he had been ashamed of it and thought it degrading and, ever since, he had lived a life of the utmost chastity." Little wonder that Augustine puts it, "These were the qualities I knew in Alypius, who was my close friend and, like myself, was perplexed to know what course of life we ought to follow."[11] To what extent did Alypius influence Augustine in "matters of sex"? It may have been considerable.

It probably was through Alypius that Augustine maintained the close tie with another family friend of long standing, Romanianus, a wealthy Roman who became Augustine's patron. Had it not been for these generous gifts, Augustine probably could not have attended the university at Carthage nor maintained his Tagaste residence: "You had already nurtured me at the beginning of my studies, you still sustained me when I wished to try my strength, and take to my wings."[12] Romanianus, "who came from my own town . . . had been one of my closest friends since boyhood,"[13] was a cousin of Alypius.

Nebridius

He was wealthy, "a young man of high principles and unexceptionable character."[14] Nebridius was born in Carthage. Augustine became his leader and mentor, source of moral and intellectual guidance. He was the youngest member of the fellowship[15] and became Augustine's intellectual companion. They shared deeply as they traveled in Africa and Italy. In later times Augustine wrote his younger colleague:

I read your letter by lamplight after dinner; it was almost time for bed, but not quite time for sleep: so I reflected for a long time, sitting on my bed, and Augustine held this conversation with Augustine. Is it not true that I am happy, as Nebridius claims?[16]

Nebridius, too, was ensnared at first, "before he was a Christian he, like us, had been caught in the pitfall of the most deadly error"[17] but that was to change and Nebridius became "a faithful Catholic." The friendship was such that later Nebridius did not hesitate to remind Augustine "you show such courage and patience in serving your fellow citizens and that the much-desired leisure is not granted you? I ask you, why do they impose on you when you are so good?"[18]

Several years later when Nebridius died, Augustine poured out his feeling:

Now he lives in Abraham's bosom, and whatever may be the meaning of that bosom, there, Nebridius lives, my very dear friend, taken by you to be your son, no longer simply one whom you had freed from bondage. There he lives. For what other place is there for a soul such as this? There he lives, in that very place about which he used to question me so much, poor ignorant man that I was.[19]

"Friendship exists only through mutual love,"[20] said Augustine. It was only natural that the first element one owes a friend is love. No service can be an act of friendship unless love be the source. "He loves his friend truly who loves God in him, either because God is in him or in order that He may be in him."[21] By loving a friend in this fashion, one avoids the danger of being overly attracted by the good in the individual, for Augustine insists that motivation for friendship must come from love for God.

With the passing of years Augustine wove the threads of church life into all other aspects of living. When expressing his feelings on what one might ask of a friend, he said, "You have asked me . . . to write something to you on the instruction of candidates for the catechumenate. . . . You have felt obliged earnestly to entreat me, by the affection I owe you, not to consider it troublesome, occupied as I am. . . . I am constrained not only by the love and service which I owe you as a friend, but also by that which I owe to our mother, the Church

. . . in no wise to refuse but rather to undertake the task with a ready and earnest will."[22]

Augustine regarded the loss of a friend one of the most painful experiences in life, along with physical suffering and death.

> What, should there be no bond of love between men? Truly there should be, so that no surer step towards God may be imagined than the love between man and man.[23]

Death of the Unnamed Friend

One friend, nameless, had been a childhood companion, "true friends." They were jointly entrapped in the Manichaean faith, "he was my companion in error and I was utterly lost without him." When the friend became gravely ill he was given the rite of Christian baptism, only to recover for a short period. Augustine made great sport of the unnecessary precaution, he "tried to chaff him about his baptism." Within a few days, "while I was away from him, the fever returned and he died." The loss was overwhelming, "I hated all the places we had known together, because he was not in them." The two had shared so many intimate conversations about their adopted Manichaeism. They had ambled up and down the steep streets of Tagaste; they had engaged others in debate in the market—a choice pasttime. "Tears alone were sweet to me, for in my heart's desire they had taken the place of my friend."[24]

Do we see here an acute single-mindedness which is a distinguishing characteristic of Augustine? Whatever he did, whatever the relationship, it tended toward the extreme—he was never nonchalant about people or ideas or events. In fact, is it not overdone? Of his friend he cried out:

> I had no hope that he would come to life again, nor was this what I begged for through my tears: I simply grieved and wept, for I was heartbroken and had lost my joy. Or is weeping, too, a bitter thing, becoming a pleasure only when things we once enjoyed turn loathsome and only as long as our dislike for them remains?[25]

One inquiry: If the friendship was so unwavering, so rarefied, why does Augustine not reveal the name? The silence is intriguing!

The question has been raised regarding Augustine's relationship with his intimate friend, and the many others who were to be so much a part of his life—was he homosexual? Or if not shown openly, was the feeling latent? His writings abound with terms of endearment addressed to men, or about men, "a friendship that was sweeter to me than all the joys of life." Is this pure rhetoric? Augustine's language was the florid style of the age; amorous terms are used with unrestraint.

At the same time, Augustine speaks of "sins against nature, therefore, like the sin of Sodom, are abominable and deserve punishment wherever and whenever they are committed."[26] He mentions "offences against human codes of conduct" and he speaks of "desecrated by perverted lust." True, these are not in a personal reference, but he makes considerable use of them. "These are the main categories of sin. They are hatched from the lust for power, from gratification of the eye, and from gratification of corrupt nature." As he speaks of sin, of unregeneracy, he does not hesitate to illustrate his point through the erogenous metaphor. Then, of a very personal nature, he states, "So I muddied the stream of friendship with the filth of lewdness and clouded its clear waters with hell's black river of lust."[27]

A few years later, in Italy, as Augustine took a strumpet from the street of Milan as a mistress, it can hardly be regarded as the activity of a homosexual. In all his writings, we see Augustine as a very physical, earthy personality who drew broadly from all phases of life, of human conduct. He employed the emotional and corporeal heavily. He was not inhibited as a writer and this is part of his genius.

In future years, as Augustine sat on his throne in his Basilica in Hippo, preaching to his people, he did not blush to depict sin in all its carnal reality. In Sermon 151 he expounded the fall of Adam and Eve who, in shame, used fig leaves to cover their genitals. He went on to speak of that identical shame which haunts believers who have no control of their sex organs, who experience nocturnal emissions. The same was true of orgasmic fantasizing, masturbatic dreams. The sex act became the badge of shame, eternal reminder of primordial rebellion against God—Augustine spelled it out in countless messages, documents, commentaries. In letters to troubled individuals he offered advice, making explicit sexual references.

Open book though it was, were there certain aspects of his life which Augustine forever kept hidden within himself? Were there secret wrestlings deep inside his makeup? What was his sexual orientation? Possibly even he did not know!

Carthage A.D. 376–383

'What madness, to love a man as something more than human!'' wrote Augustine as he recalled the appalling remorse at his friend's death. "The god I worshipped was my own delusion, and if I tried to find in it a place to rest my burden, there was nothing there to uphold it.'' In desperation "my eyes were less tempted to look for my friend in a place where they had not grown used to seeing him. So from Tagaste I went to Carthage."[28]

Returning to Carthage was inevitable. Tagaste was too small and its provincialism limited a budding career. In 376, at age twenty-two, Augustine became a professional teacher of rhetoric—operating a "word shop" as he called it—in the capital of Africa. Carthage, second only to Rome in the Western world, was a strategic spot. It was also an auspicious time to be in Carthage, for the son and son-in-law of Ausonius, favorite and tutor of young Emperor Theodosius I, had been named proconsuls. Ausonius had been an orator, hence there was an increased respect for men holding that professional standing. Likewise another former orator and official, Symmachus, now a Roman senator, maintained a substantial villa in the city. There were numerous other distinguished Romans, men of letters and affairs. These were wealthy men and they could become patrons for a young orator who demonstrated talent. Many possibilities were at hand whereby one might become rich, and be liberated from toil. This had developed into an ideal for many lazy, intellectual Romans—"a country estate, a house, gardens watered by clear streams, the soft glow of marble in contrasting shades. To live this way helps me towards a quiet old age, turning over the learned writings of the ancient masters."[29] It was Augustine's dream, and, in a sense, it never changed, not even when he was an old man. He always enjoyed luxurious retreats from the humdrum, as when he dined on peacock while attending a meeting in Carthage.

Augustine seems to have been eminently successful, as orator and congenial associate of important Carthaginians. One such individual was "that wise old man Vindicianus,"[30] who proved to be exceedingly helpful. It was a stroke of luck for Augustine. Vindicianus was "a man of deep understanding, who had an excellent reputation for his great skill as a doctor. As he was proconsul at the time, his was the hand that laid upon my head the wreath I won in the poetry competition."[31] Among his several contributions to Augustine was a warning against astrology. He was "quite outspoken on the subject" and Augustine regarded it God's doing, "you did not fail to use even that old man to help me."

Another who, unwittingly, was "to cure my obstinacy" was Firminus, who "had been educated in the liberal arts and had received a thorough training in rhetoric." Firminus claimed to be an authority on astrology. He described minutely the story of his own birth and that of a slave—both born at exactly the same moment—and how their horoscopes calculated the future. "Taking this as my starting point I began to think the matter over in my mind." As Augustine pondered the issue he thought of Esau and Jacob. To foretell their futures could have been pure luck. "By now, O God my Help, you had released me by this means from the bondage of astrology."

More success: at age twenty-six Augustine became an author. It was probably in 380, the year Vindicianus became proconsul that Augustine wrote his first book *Beauty and Proportion*, unfortunately no longer extant. Later in Hippo, Augustine himself was unable to locate a copy. This pastiche, a work on aesthetics, was dedicated to a noted orator in Rome, "what induced me to dedicate my book to Hierius, the great public speaker at Rome?" The answer is simple: Augustine wanted attention. "I had never even seen him, but I admired his brilliant reputation for learning and had been greatly struck by what I had heard of his speeches. . . . I was impressed by the admiration which other people had for him."[32] Hierius was "born in Syria and originally trained to speak in Greek, had later become so remarkable a speaker in Latin, and had also such a wealth of knowledge of the subjects studied by philosophers." Such was Augustine's new world, and his heroes were those who had gained wealth and fame as intellectuals. It was the life of the dilettante, and Augustine's lost volume in all likelihood reflected it. It may be just as well that it is safe in oblivion.

Disillusion was gradually falling upon Augustine as he vainly attempted to discover substantive purpose in his Manichaean faith. He was searching at a deeper level, asking, seeking, and the Manichees were now quite unable to answer. His interest in philosophy had never waned. "When I was only about twenty years of age Aristotle's book on the 'Ten Categories' came into my hands." How stimulating to find that when "My teacher at Carthage and others who were reputed to be scholars mentioned this book, their cheeks would swell with self-importance." He stood agape, knowing he was poised on the threshold of some "divine mystery." Lo, "I managed to read it and understand it without help."[33] He likewise "read and understood by myself all the books that I could find on the so-called liberal arts."[34] He was growing intellectually and it is no surprise that in "the twenty-ninth year of my age" the change came.

"A Manichaean bishop named Faustus had recently arrived in Carthage . . . many people were trapped by his charming manner of speech."[35] Yet more, "Manichees talked so much about this man Faustus that I wanted to see what scholarly fare he would lay before me."[36] It was the great opportunity to discover the ultimate truth in Manichaean thought. Augustine had long anticipated Faustus of Mileve, a Numidian of real intellect. It was the moment of truth. "As soon as it became clear to me that Faustus was quite uninformed about the subjects in which I had expected him to be an expert, I began to lose hope." The end had really come. Manichaeism proved to be bankrupt. "Of course, despite his ignorance of these matters he might still have been a truly pious man, provided he were not a Manichee." Augustine had been outgrowing the ideas for some years. Now came the full realization that as a life faith it had proved to be a fraud. At best it would be regarded as a passing fad. "The keen interest which I had had in Manichaean doctrines was checked by this experience . . . unwittingly and without intent, Faustus who had been a deadly snare to many now began to release me from the trap."

Another change was in the offing. "It was, then, . . . that I was persuaded to go to Rome and teach there the subjects which I taught at Carthage."[37] Larger fees were to be had in Rome, and certainly it was the preeminent post. Augustine says, however, that the real motive for going, "almost the only one, . . . [was that] the behaviour of the young students at Rome was quieter. Discipline was stricter and they were not permitted to rush insolently and just as they pleased into the lecture-rooms." His Carthaginian students were beyond control; their action disgraceful. "They come blustering into the lecture-room like a troop of maniacs and upset the orderly arrangements which the master has made in the interest of his pupils. Their recklessness is unbelievable."

While Augustine may have protested the gross behavior, in reality Rome was a necessity, and his life situation, not African students, prescribed a fresh impetus. If he was to reach the pinnacle as a rhetorician, Italy afforded the opportunity. But more, while he does not say so, he was an adult who needed to be free, with the Mediterranean separating him from Monica's domination.

Most memorable in Augustine's departure was the deception perpetrated—by necessity—upon Monica. She had followed her son with a hyena-like tenacity from Tagaste to Carthage. Now, "She wept bitterly to see me go and followed me to the water's edge, clinging to me with all her strength in the hope that I would either come home or take her with me." In order to escape, the twenty-nine-year-old son "deceived her with the excuse that I had a friend whom I did not want to leave until the wind rose and his ship could sail. It was a lie."

Monica refused to budge, but was willing to spend the night at the shrine of the great African martyr Cyprian. "During the night, secretly, I sailed away." The umbilical cord was finally severed! Was it not high time he set out on his own? In retrospect he regarded her tears as "water that would wash me clean." He would always have her at his side, but now he was trying his own wings—a new setting. "The wind blew and filled our sails, and the shore disappeared from sight."[38]

Indeed, the following morning Monica was "wild with grief," her anticipated dreams shattered—momentarily. "For as mothers do, and far more than most, she loved to have me with her." Overcome, she "wept and wailed, and the torments which she suffered were proof that she had inherited the legacy of Eve, seeing in sorrow what with sorrow she had brought into the world." Eventually she calmed, accepted her son's "deceit and cruelty" with prayer and fortitude. "She went back to her house, and I went on to Rome." It is intriguing that in describing the highly charged scene with Monica, and his subsequent guilt-ridden departure, Augustine says nothing of leaving the loving mistress and young Adeodatus. Apparently saying good-bye to them was far less emotional, perhaps a matter-of-fact withdrawal.

Melodramatically Augustine took leave of Carthage, but he could never forget the city. In coming years it was to play a major part in his career. As an adult he visited Carthage some thirty times; the city was forever appearing in his writings:

> When indeed I wish to speak of Carthage, I seek within myself what to speak, and I find within myself an image of Carthage; but I have received this through the body, that is through the senses of the body, since I have been present in that city . . . I saw and perceived it, and retained it in my memory . . . its word is the image itself of it in my memory, not that sound or two syllables when Carthage is named.[39]

Or, "Again when I call to mind some arch of beautiful and symmetrical lines which I saw, let us say, at Carthage."[40]

VI
Italy

The Eternal City A.D. 383

"You applied the spur . . . that would draw me to Rome."[1] It was a city of a million and a quarter inhabitants. No longer official residence of the Imperial Court, its glory was mixed with nostalgia. There was the Forum with its columns, the gilded statues, marble steps, and three thousand palaces of the plutocrats—many with incomes exceeding two million in gold a year. It was magnificent. Rome was also squalor. Slaves and plebeians existed in jammed dwellings—fire traps —several stories high, reached by ladders, for which exorbitant rents were charged.

Augustine found lodgings with a Manichee (he made use of his ties), in the Velabrum quarter where immigrants from Egypt, the Levantine countries, and the Orient fought against disease and filth. Nearby were the great warehouses on the Tiber.

"I was at once struck down by illness, which all but carried me off to hell." It was touch and go, "My fever rose. I came close to dying," and all the while Monica, knowing nothing of the particular malady, was remembering "to pray for me." In due time Augustine improved; "you healed my sickness." Hardly a promising beginning. Yet Augustine was in Rome, and to whom did he turn in his hour of need? "In Rome I did not part company with those would-be saints . . . one of whom was my host during my illness and convalescence." The die may have been cast, his faith in the Manichees shattered, yet "I remained on more familiar terms," probably because he knew no one else and he had no qualms about accepting hospitality from those he secretly rejected. He laughed at this grotesque cult, yet he used it.

It was a disappointing year in Rome, especially "the business of teaching literature and public speaking." Augustine may have found his own place in the African section. "At first I taught in my house," and there was a pleasing response, but a rude awakening; Roman students were not like Carthaginians. "No rioting by young hooligans" but a new ploy, "a number of students would plot together to avoid paying their master his fees and would transfer in a body to another." He both hated and loved these students, an ambivalence he speaks of with candor: "But in those days I was readier to dislike them for fear of the harm they might cause me."

Any orator coming to Rome took a chance. Fortunately a substantial opportunity presented itself in the person of Symmachus, Prefect of the City, who noticed this new African and liked him. An opening came, not in the City of the Caesars, but a real plum: a professor of rhetoric was needed for the city of Milan. This post would be under the scrutiny of the Imperial Court itself, and the Orator would deliver the official panegyrics on the Emperor:

> So, when the Prefect of Rome received a request from Milan to find a teacher of literature and elocution for the city, with a promise that travelling expenses would be charged to public funds, I applied for the appointment, armed with recommendations from my friends who were so fuddled with the Manichaean rigmarole. . . . Eventually Symmachus . . . set me a test to satisfy himself of my abilities and sent me to Milan.[2]

Again Augustine benefited from the Manichees; without their aid the position might have gone to others. Now it was Milan, residence of the Emperor Valentinian II, and it came, in part, as the last favor received from the hands of those he resented, a parting gift—donors unaware of the parting—from erstwhile friends. They provided adequate testimonials. In their eyes his credentials were impeccable.

Augustine's greatest opportunity lay before him; he was filled with expectation. "God, by deferring our hope, stretches our desire; by the desiring, stretches the mind; by stretching, makes it more capacious."[3] He also wrote of the stress, "When men seek God and strain their minds to the capacity of human weakness to arrive at an understanding, having learnt by experience the wearisome difficulties of the task."[4] He was speaking here of the search within Scripture, but in a broader context he may have had in mind life's quest. He was taking another step.

Milan A.D. 384–386

"In Milan I found your devoted servant Ambrose."[5] More to the point, Augustine found himself, but it was a lengthy process, begun in Carthage with the *Hortensius*, and continuing under the preaching of this prince of the pulpit.

Augustine turned again to philosophy, reading the Academics, sceptics who brilliantly opposed the Stoics and their view that man could comprehend the world. "I began to think [the] . . . Academics were wiser than the rest, . . . everything was a matter of doubt . . . man can know nothing for certain."[6] It fit his present situation, for it became clear that the Manichees with their "ready-made" Wisdom posed a too-easy solution. Obtaining real wisdom was a lifetime quest; false opinions had to be jettisoned.[7] For his own satisfaction, Augustine reviewed those absurd Manichaean views: God having "the shape of a human body . . . limited within the dimensions of limbs like our own. . . . For the same reason I believed that evil, too, was some similar kind of substance, a shapeless, hideous mass, which might be solid, in which case the Manichees called it earth, or fine and rarefied like air . . . a kind of evil mind filtering through the substance they call earth."[8]

How does one find truth? Eternal Truth? "I had lost hope that man could find the path." He did not abandon the struggle, rather "treating everything as a matter of doubt, as the Academics are generally supposed to do, and hovering between one doctrine and another, I made up my mind at least to leave the Manichees. . . . I found the theories of some of the philosophers preferable." Still, unable to trust the Academics completely, he finally "decided to remain a catechumen,"[9] at least for the time being. It was what his parents had wanted. He was not a Catholic but was willing to be instructed in the rudiments of the faith.

Ambrose

Of the many contributors in the Milan experience, Ambrose is the most important. For eleven years prior to Augustine's coming, Ambrose had served as Bishop of Milan. Fourteen years older than the

orator from Africa, a patrician by birth and personality, Ambrose was
a man of authority. He was a cousin of the pagan Symmachus who
had appointed Augustine. As gifted in administration as he was in
preaching, Ambrose demanded and received the respect of the Emperor Theodosius. "Nothing vulgar, nothing popular, nothing in
common with the ambitions and customs and manners of the rude
multitude, is expected in priests," he wrote. "The dignity of the
priesthood demands a sober and elevated calmness, a serious life, a
special gravity."[10]

"This man of God received me like a father"[11] recalled Augustine, but it was a stern, puritan patriarch. When Ambrose was in his
pulpit, "I listened attentively . . . for my purpose . . . whether the
reports of his powers as a speaker were accurate . . . I was delighted
with his charming delivery." So it was one elocutionist coming to
judge another. A personal visit was another matter. "We found him
reading . . . we would sit quietly, for no one had the heart to disturb
him."[12] And how could they do otherwise? Who had the affrontive-
ness to barge in? Ambrose was the type man Augustine needed; their
meeting was wholly appropriate: reserved, restrained. Augustine did
not need emotional people to fall upon his neck proffering artificial
friendship.

Ambrose was a superb preacher who employed a fresh style, an ex-
egetical method whereby he discovered and used subtle allegory. What
a gratification to see the Old Testament "in a different light . . . he
lifted the veil of mystery and disclosed the spiritual meaning of texts."
There were so many questions, "I wanted to be equally sure [of] . . .
both material things . . . and spiritual things." Augustine's psyche was
still infested with the Gnostic-Manichaean idea that all flesh was evil.
Ambrose presented a glorious new concept, and Augustine was "influenced by an authoritative statement, and prepared to say that there was
something 'immaterial,' but unable to think other than in terms taken
from material things."[13] How Ambrose must have enraptured his flock
with sermons from The Song of Solomon.

We witness a gradual unfolding, the "evolution of a metaphysi-
cian" as Augustine moved to the acceptance of spiritual reality. "All
the time I had been telling myself one tale after another." He outlined
his intellectual, spiritual autobiography:

Tomorrow I shall discover the truth. I shall see it quite plainly, and it will be mine to keep . . .

Faustus will come and explain everything . . .

The Academics! What wonderful men they are! Is it true that we can never know for certain how we ought to manage our lives . . .?

No, not that! We must search all the more carefully . . .

Great hope is born in me, because I have found that the doctrines of the Catholic faith are not what I thought them to be . . . Why then do I hesitate to knock. . .?

Suppose death puts an end to all care . . .

As I reasoned with myself . . . my heart was buffeted.[14]

At this juncture Monica arrived in Milan, late spring of A.D. 385, having seen to property she inherited from Patricius. With her was Navigius, her eldest son, and two nephews, Rusticus and Lastidianus. Nebridius was also in the party. This African phalanstery moved in with Augustine and he was expected to provide for all, no small order for a speech professor just establishing himself. He was already head of a small African colony, for his concubine and Adeodatus were in the household, and Alypius had come from the homeland. Such an exodus was not uncommon for Africans. Their arrival, joyful as it may have been, was likewise the source of far-reaching, none too happy consequences. Monica's presence usually precipitated rich family laughter—and concomitant tears.

"By now my mother had come to me."[15] Her piety and courage had been observed on the ship, which had been "in danger," but "it was she who put heart into the crew." Like Paul, she "promised them that they would make the land in safety," for a vision had been given her.

Ambrose and his celebrated church became a focal point in Monica's life in Milan. At first she thought to continue her African custom "to take meal-cakes and bread and wine to the shrines of the saints on their memorial days," but Ambrose put a stop to it. Surprisingly, she continued to be "greatly devoted to Ambrose" and the bishop reciprocated. "He would break out in praise of her, congratulating me on having such a mother."[16]

Augustine describes a dramatic, hair-raising experience in Milan:

> It was only a year, or not much more, since Justina, the mother
> of the boy emperor Valentinian, had been persecuting your de-
> voted servant Ambrose in the interests of heresy into which the
> Arians had seduced her. In those days your faithful people used
> to keep watch in the church, ready to die with their bishop, your
> servant. My mother, your handmaid, was there with them, tak-
> ing a leading part in the anxious time of vigilance and living a
> life of constant prayer.[17]

Yea, Monica was in her element, and she loved it.

It becomes quite natural that a turning point—again—had come for
Augustine: "From now on I began to prefer the Catholic teaching."[18]
Monica's proximity had always provided a powerful influence, and
there had been an incipient alteration prior to her arrival. While she
was not wholly responsible for the move toward Catholicism, her presence helped. Ambrose had provided theological substance and biblical
interpretation which was of tremendous value. And Augustine knew it.

Perhaps it was Monica's strict moralistic view which brought about
the break; perchance it was something Ambrose said; or maybe it was
the stirrings of conscience. A decision was made regarding the mother
of Adeodatus: she had to leave. As Augustine had mused about Ambrose he noted, "His celibacy seemed to me the only hardship which
he had to bear." Far more, Augustine was now in deep anguish about
the woman with whom he had lived for some fifteen years. We can
never forget his baleful cry of dereliction:

> Meanwhile I was sinning more and more. The woman with
> whom I had been living was torn from my side as an obstacle to
> my marriage and this was a blow which crushed my heart to
> bleeding, because I loved her dearly. She went back to Africa,
> vowing never to give herself to any other man, and left with me
> the son whom she had borne me.[19]

A marriage, doubtless arranged—at least in part—by Monica to an
heiress from one of the best families in Milan was one of several necessary steps to rise in upper-class circles in Italy. There had to be a two-
year waiting period as the bride was not yet of age. Since fourteen was
nubile age, the girl must have been but twelve. This would be sufficient
time to get the concubine out of the picture, and out of mind.

No question about it, the moral view of the day—both Roman and

Catholic—regarded casting aside a mistress rather as a matter of course; it was "not bigamy, but a sign of moral improvement,"[20] especially for a man advancing in the world.

Monica was a child of her age as well as a mother apprehensive about her son's future. Her dominance in the home springs from an African dictum that if a man's mother and wife were together in a sinking boat, which of the two would he save? His mother! Wives can be replaced, mothers never. Possibly we can understand the action by Augustine and Monica, but hardly condone. Neither can we look with favor upon writers—a host—who hasten to defend Augustine, making him a plastic, pious, spiritless dolt. Abandoning the concubine, with an eye to a decorous marriage, was tolerated in the fourth century. Obviously, the woman was cruelly abused. Why could she not have become Augustine's lawful spouse? She becomes token of a culture, a time, a value system, "More sinn'd against than sinning." And what, pray tell, did it do to her, to give up husband, son, home? And what of Adeodatus? He was twelve and saw his mother go. His woe? And Augustine never reveals her name!

During the period immediately following his woman's departure it all struck home to the wretched Augustine. "I was impatient at the delay of two years which had to pass before the girl whom I had asked to marry became my wife, and because I was more a slave of lust than a true lover of marriage, I took another mistress, without sanction of wedlock."[21] A slut?

Augustine's famous supplication, set in the context of "early adolescence," may more rightly be placed at this traumatic juncture: "Give me chastity and continence, but not yet."[22] A loving woman discarded; a whore to sleep with; burning passion and tortured conscience: it was hell.

Is it from his own experience that he later established Catholic rule: "Married people owe each other not only the fidelity of sexual intercourse for the purpose of procreating children—and this is the first association of the human race in this mortal life—but also the mutual service, . . . of sustaining each other's weakness, for the avoidance of illicit intercourse. . . . In marriage, intercourse for the purpose of generation has no fault attached to it, but for the purpose of satisfying concupiscence, provided with a spouse, because of the marriage fidelity, it is a venial sin; adultery or fornication, however, is a mortal sin. And so, continence from all intercourse is certainly better than marital intercourse itself which takes place for the sake of begetting children."[23]

As he grew older Augustine continued to write on marriage, and increasingly, marriage, as personal friendship, must be seen in the light of faith in God. He advised women:

> A husband and wife love each other because they see each other, and they fear in each other what they do not see. They do not rejoice with certainty from that which is evident, since they suspect in secret what, for the most part, does not exist.
>
> You, in Him whom you do not behold with your eyes, but contemplate by faith, do not find anything true of which you will disapprove; nor do you fear that perhaps you will offend Him by something falsely alleged.
>
> If, therefore, you owed great love to husbands, how much ought you to love Him for whose sake you have chosen not to have husbands! Let Him be placed in complete possession of your heart, who for you was placed upon the cross; let Him possess entirely within your soul whatever you did not wish to be usurped by marriage. It is not lawful for you to love sparingly Him for whose sake you did not love even what was lawful. I have no fear of pride in you who so love Him who is meek and humble of heart.[24]

Did he ever erase her from his mind? Why so much talk of marriage?

> Furthermore the wound that I had received when my first mistress was wrenched away showed no signs of healing. At first the pain was sharp and searing, but then the wound began to fester, and though the pain was duller there was all the less hope of a cure.[25]

There is a traditional story that, on leaving, the mistress remarked that she would never be able to love again. She could not love even a Caesar, having once known the love of Augustine. Did she ever read Augustine's *Confessions*?

Plotinus and the Platonists

During the months in Milan, A.D. 385–386, while Augustine was living in a scholarly environment, it was a time of serious thinking. He

now craved pensive re-examination of his personal conflicts, his heavy
sense of sin and guilt. He also yearned for continued intellectual stimu-
lation. He was surrounded by friends who enjoyed the studious life;
philosophy dominated their daily conversations. The wealthy Romanianus was now in Milan due to a protracted lawsuit and of course he was
a member of Augustine's company. The novel idea came: why not create a retreat? "We were like three hungry mouths. . . . Again and
again we asked ourselves this question, but we did not relinquish our
worldly aims, because we could not see the light of any truth that we
might grasp in place of them."[26] Augustine had always been attracted
to that contemplative leisure which he saw among the rich in Africa,
Rome, and Milan. This would be true felicity. Would such a community not be ideal? Oh, how he looked with envy on a happy beggar:

> As I walked along one of the streets in Milan I noticed a poor
> beggar who must, I suppose, have had his fill of food and drink,
> since he was laughing and joking. Sadly I turned to my com-
> panions and spoke to them of all the pain and trouble which is
> caused by our own folly. My ambitions had placed a load of
> misery on my shoulders and the further I carried it the heavier it
> became, but the only purpose of all the efforts we made was to
> reach the goal of peaceful happiness. This beggar had already
> reached it ahead of us, and perhaps we should never reach it at
> all.[27]

Where is happiness? Who is happy? "My soul, then, must beware of
those who say that what matters is the reason why a man is happy."

It could not have come at a more appropriate time: the rediscovery
of Plato. The writings of that prince of philosophers were now much in
vogue, and Augustine and his associates were totally caught up in this
exciting new mania. They were devotees of the greatest of Greek philosophers, whose works had been rediscovered a century earlier
through the writings of the Egyptian Greek, Plotinus. His *Enneads*, edited by his Greek disciple Porphyry, became standard reading for intellectuals who made any claim to a knowledge of philosophy. The term
used today, Neo-Platonism—coined in the nineteenth century—would
have been laughed at by Augustine. He would have insisted on being
called a Platonist. He had no interest in somebody's interpretation of
the Greek genius; it was Plato himself who was the fountainhead, "the
most refined and enlightened."[28] Augustine even had a dream about

philosophy in which a "man explained to him a number of points in Plato, which he had formerly refused to explain."[29]

Plotinus would not have been looked upon as a latter-day scholar, one who was only an interpreter of Plato. Rather he was seen as one who brought a pure Plato to the student. "Now we selected the Platonists as being deservedly the best known of all philosophers, because they have been able to realize that the soul of man, though immortal and rational (or intellectual) cannot attain happiness except by participation in the light of God, the creator of the soul and of the whole world."[30] Augustine speaks, in glowing terms, how "Plotinus often stresses . . . that even the being whom they hold to be the 'Soul of the Universe' receives its blessedness from the source of our soul's felicity; and that source is the light, direct from the Soul itself, by which it was created and by whose intelligible illumination it shines with intelligible light."[31]

Plotinus was interpreted and edited by the faithful Porphyry, and his works include *On the Life of Plotinus* and *Life of Plotinus*. It was Porphyry who fashioned a theological system out of Plotinus' view of Plato, or perhaps better to say Plotinus' discovery of Plato. Augustine held Porphyry in high esteem, as one "in subjection to those envious powers, and [who] was at the same time ashamed of his subjection and yet afraid to contradict them openly." Augustine observed, "It was of course his pride which blinded Porphyry."[32]

Augustine's introduction to Plato, as to Cicero, was a blessing. He had yearned for illumination; he was now overjoyed. The newfound treasure was not contemplated as philosophy in the guise of old, pagan Greek philosophy of Athens, but rather was venerated in a Christian context in Milan. Augustine was revering Plato as a near-Christian. "If those things which Plato and Plotinus said about God are true, is it enough for you to know God as they knew Him?"[33] Another voice: that of Marius Victorinus, an African teacher of rhetoric in Rome in the middle of the century, had joined the Catholic Church. He also set out to translate Plotinus and Porphyry into Latin. Victorinus was a friend of the aged and highly respected Simplicianus of Milan. It was Simplicianus who taught Ambrose. Plato was thus safely in Christian hands and the Catholic Church was avidly attempting to combine Platonism and Christian theology. Augustine moved into this ready-made situa-

tion, "So I went to Simplicianus, the spiritual father of Ambrose. . . . I
told him how I had drifted from error to error, and when I mentioned
that I had read some of the books of the Platonists translated into Latin
by Victorinus, who had once been professor of rhetoric at Rome. . .
Simplicianus said that he was glad that I had not stumbled upon the
writings of other philosophers," for he held that they were . . . "full of
fallacies and misrepresentations *drawn from worldly principles.*"[34]
Here was another personality, a man who spoke to Augustine's condition. He joyfully continued, "In the Platonists, he said, God and his
Word are constantly implied. Then, to encourage me to follow Christ's
example of humility, . . . he told me about Victorinus, whom he had
known intimately when he was in Rome."

Augustine was astonished as he listened to the pagan honors which
had been thrust upon his fellow African, Victorinus, a truly redoubted
orator, "of great learning, with a profound knowledge of all the liberal
sciences. He had studied a great many books of philosophy and published criticisms of them. He had been master to many distinguished
members of the Senate, . . . and had even been awarded a statue in the
Roman forum—a great honour in the eyes of the world." A rank pagan, he had read the Scriptures and "made the most painstaking and
careful study of all Christian literature." He frequently said to Simplicianus, "I want you to know that I am now a Christian." To which
Simplicianus replied, "I shall not believe it or count you as a Christian
until I see you in the Church of Christ." To this came the laughing reply, "Is it then the walls of the church that make the Christian?"[35]
Eventually the popular Victorinus "made his declaration of the true
faith with splendid confidence." And it was not made in private, but
publically. Was he not an orator? It was his grandest moment. Augustine was overcome in hearing the story.

Augustine read Plato in translations, "some of the books of the
Platonists, translated from Greek into Latin. In them I read—not, of
course, word for word, though the sense was the same and it was supported by all kinds of different arguments."[36] The Platonists, Augustine found, resolved some of the ideas of Plato and Aristotle. They
created in the process what Augustine called "the one absolutely true
philosophical culture."[37] Next, he discovered that Platonism and the
gospel were joined. Plato's Ideals were not in conflict with "And the

Logos was made flesh." This is what all the Christian Platonists were saying.

Were these Christian philosophers of Milan really true to Plato? Perhaps not in the strict sense of classic Greek studies, but they would never admit it. Ambrose looked upon students of Plato as "aristocrats of thought."[38] Let the scholars in Athens and Alexandria smile if they wish. Students in northern Italy were wrestling with Truth and Salvation.

Augustine was now engrossed in Plato quite as much as his teacher-preacher, Ambrose. Ideas were being assimilated in an unbelievable manner. He notes that at this point "My thoughts ranged only amongst material forms. I defined them in two classes, those which please the eye because they are beautiful in themselves and those which do so because they are properly proportioned in relation to something else." He quickly moves from physical considerations of line and colour and shape, to metaphysics, observing, "since my soul had no such visible qualities, I argued that I could not see it."[39]

Plotinus held that the universe had a center. However, the frail mind of man could not really grasp it. All about man is the clutter of his attempts to construct a whole universe. Man lives in a world of sense, and what is he doing? He is slowly drifting, in a "progression of declining stages of awareness," with each stage of awareness seeking to touch the superior stage just above it. There is a remarkably compelling tension here between the movement of the One going out from the Center—and the attempt of every part to come back, to return to the source of consciousness. The Intellect, as Plotinus viewed it, was the all important Mediating Principle. Augustine read all of this and saw the gospel expressed in it. He thus acknowledged, "Though the words were different and the meaning was expressed in various ways, I also learned from these books that God the Son, being himself, like the Father, of divine nature,"[40] proceeded. He saw the intellect as a yearning to be complete.

"Procession" in Plotinus was the outward movement. From the One there was a flowing, like the heat of the African sun. Each being draws strength from the One, just as all creatures gather strength from the sun. Then there is the "Turning" inward movement. Although God had seemed remote to Augustine, we now see him "turning." "Eternal

Truth, true Love, beloved Eternity—all this, my God, you are, and it is to you that I sigh by night and day. . . . Your light shone upon me in its brilliance, and I thrilled with love and dread alike. . . . And, far off, I heard your voice saying *I am the God who IS* . . . and at once I had no cause to doubt."[41]

It was the problem of evil which was again troubling Augustine:

> For you evil does not exist, and not only for you but for the whole of your creation as well, because there is nothing outside it which could invade it and break down the order which you have imposed on it. Yet in the separate parts of your creation there are some things which we think of as evil because they are at variance with other things. But there are other things again with which they are in accord, and then they are good. . . . And since this is so, I no longer wished for a better world, because I was thinking of the whole of creation. . . . Though the higher things are better than the lower, the sum of all creation is better than the higher things alone.[42]

Immersed as he was in Plato, Augustine was discovering that philosophy, not literature per se, was the best atmosphere for intellectual life and breath. He experienced a metamorphosis: no longer was there merely scepticism of the New Academy. He delighted in contending with the "pagan" Platonists in the Milan arena—brilliant philosophers who were repulsed by all references to a *body*—Incarnation, Crucifixion, Resurrection. "If only," he argued, "you had been able to see his incarnation, in which he took a human soul and body, as the supreme instance of grace."[43]

Augustine's intellectual appetite was whetted; he longed for more food for soul and mind. He welcomed any opportunity to share in the community of thinkers, yet something was lacking. An inner conflict was yet to be resolved. An older Augustine would say in later years, "My desire is insufficient, unless in that which I have desired, You yourself led me." He also confessed:

> Because it is You who made me, let it not be Your will to destroy me utterly. Scourge me so that I may be made better, not so that I cease to be; beat me so that I may be given a better shape, not so as to crush me to bits.[44]

By late summer Augustine reached a point of no return. Long he had grappled with himself, with ideas; he had read extensively and spent hours in heady discussions. He had probed, analyzed, known heartache. "God willed that even in the matter of perseverance in goodness itself," he once wrote, "His saints should not glory in their own strength, but in Himself, who not only gives them aid . . . [but] without which they cannot persevere."[45] Indeed, it was perseverance. Years later, as an old Augustine reviewed his lifework, he reverently observed, "Man must first be restored to himself, that, making in himself as it were a stepping-stone, he may rise thence and be borne up to God."[46]

VII
Conversion

The Garden in Milan, September A.D. 386

"This was the nature of my sickness. I was tormented, reproaching myself more bitterly than ever as I twisted and turned in my chain." Again, "My lower instincts . . . were stronger than the higher." Augustine tells of the frightful struggle: his animalistic passions were enticing, luring his tortured sexual being.

> They plucked at my garment of flesh and whispered, 'Are you going to dismiss us? From this moment we shall never be with you again, for ever and ever. From this moment you will never again be allowed to do this thing or that, for evermore.'

Could he renounce sexual pleasure—never to revel in it again? "Close your ears to the unclean whispers of your body."[1]

In August of 386 an African, Ponticianus, "who held a high position in the Emperor's household," visited Augustine and "happened to notice a book lying on a table. . . . He picked it up and opened it and was greatly surprised to find that it contained Paul's epistles . . . he smiled and looked at me and said how glad he was." Augustine had searched Paul's writings diligently, but for all his effort the hoped-for goal eluded him. He mentioned to Ponticianus his interest in the Egyptian monk Anthony, whereupon Ponticianus described his own experience of God's forgiving power. He, too, had been spellbound by the biography of Anthony. Three of his associates had quite literally been converted at Treves, completely renouncing worldliness—including marriage.

Augustine was flabbergasted. "All the time that Ponticianus was

speaking my conscience gnawed away at me like this. I was overcome
by burning shame, and when he had finished his tale and completed the
business for which he had come, he went away and I was left to my
own thoughts." In bitter anguish Augustine cudgeled and belaboured
his own soul, only to discover "it fought back. It would not obey and
yet could offer no excuse."

It was a September day. Augustine and Alypius were alone. A garden joined their house, and it was here, under a fig tree, that much of
their reading was enjoyed. There was no enjoyment in the garden that
day, only torment for Augustine. "My inner self was a house divided
against itself. . . . I turned upon Alypius. . . . 'What is the matter with
us?' " It was too much. "I now found myself driven by the tumult in
my breast to take refuge in the garden where no one could interrupt that
fierce struggle, in which I was my own contestant, until it came to its
conclusion."[2]

Alypius wisely remained silent as Augustine flung himself under
the fig tree. "I was frantic, overcome by violent anger with myself for
not accepting your will and entering into your covenant. Yet in my
bones I knew that this was what I ought to do. . . . I performed many
bodily actions. . . . I tore my hair and hammered my forehead with my
fists; I locked my fingers and hugged my knees." He sardonically recalled the feckless Manichees who would blithely chatter, "Clearly he
has two natures, the good one bringing him here to us and the bad one
leading him away. Otherwise, how can you explain this dilemma of
two opposing wills?" He had heard it so often: "It was part of the punishment of a sin freely committed by Adam, my first father." Oh, yes,
"The weight I carried was the habit of the flesh."

Weeping copiously, Augustine continued his Gethsemane: was he
willing to let his carnal self die? Suddenly it came, the words, "Take it
and read; take it and read." It was quite clear:

> All at once I heard the sing-song voice of a child in a nearby
> house. Whether it was the voice of a boy or a girl I cannot say,
> but again and again it repeated the refrain "Take it and read,
> take it and read." At this I looked up, thinking hard whether
> there was any kind of game in which children used to chant
> words like these, but I could not remember ever hearing them
> before.[3]

This was the moment—the culmination of a lifetime pursuit! He was entering a new realm:

> I stemmed my flood of tears and stood up, telling myself that this could only be a divine command to open my book of Scripture and read the first passage on which my eyes should fall. For I had heard the story of Anthony . . . how he had happened to go into a church while the Gospel was being read and had taken it as counsel. . . . So I hurried back to the place where Alypius was sitting, for when I stood up to move away I had put down the book containing Paul's Epistles. I seized it and opened it, and in silence I read the first passage on which my eyes fell.

The text was Romans 13:13: "not in revelling and drunkenness, not in lust and wantonness, not in quarrels and rivalries. Rather, arm yourselves with the Lord Jesus Christ; spend no more thought on nature and nature's appetites." Why did he open the volume to this of all passages? Had he read and re-read it until the worn pages fell open, almost by themselves?

> I had no wish to read more and no need to do so. For in an instant, as I came to the end of the sentence, it was as though the light of confidence flooded into my heart and all the darkness of doubt was dispelled.

Marking the place, Augustine calmly looked at Alypius; together they quietly re-read the passage. As Alypius read he "applied this to himself." They then walked into the house to tell Monica, "who was overjoyed." As they described the experience she was "jubilant with triumph." Augustine summed it up as God's doing completely:

> You converted me to yourself, so that I no longer desired a wife or placed any hope in this world but stood firmly upon the rule of faith, where you had shown me to her in a dream so many years before.

What was it? The garden experience has been exploited by some Augustine writers, blissfully overlooked by others. It cannot be neglected. It has been suggested that the Latin *tolle lege*—"Take it and read"—came from the missionary church of the day, a formal phrase used before the reading of Scripture, a summons to "take Scripture, receive the word of God, and be converted."[4] Perhaps the voice Augustine heard was that of the choir—possibly a children's choir—at Ambrose's church, rehearsing the liturgy used before the reading of Scripture. It was, after all, in Milan that chanting became an important part of Christian liturgy. Music in Ambrose's services had attracted Augustine from the very first; he reveled in it. Was the chanting now speaking to him?

A clear decision was made, "Now that I had been redeemed by you I had no intention of offering myself for sale again."[5] What was the decision? "At last my mind was free from the gnawing anxieties of ambition and gain, from wallowing in filth and scratching the itching sore of lust." Where does it begin? "The mind gives an order to the body and is at once obeyed.... The mind commands the hand to move.... The mind orders itself to make an act of will.... For the will commands that an act of will should be made.... The reason, then, why the command is not obeyed is that it is not given with the full will."[6] Indeed the decision was of will. It was complete surrender, but was it Augustine's doing? "During all those years, where was my free will?" Was it accomplished in Augustine's own strength? Never! "How sweet all at once it was for me to be rid of those fruitless joys.... You drove them from me and took their place."[7] It was God's act, a gracious act.

By the grace of God, Aurelius Augustinus was made conscious of new selfhood. His will was in God's hands and he was now to serve God's purpose. What of sex, the prime area of personal frustration? He claimed it .was now transformed to a consuming passion to serve Christ. Was it thus transformed, or was it transferred?

Philosophical wrestling had helped enormously to pave the way for spiritual and intellectual change, and now the transformation had come. It was a moment of high emotion: joy! The garden in Milan becomes the bench mark in Augustine's life. Indeed, it is one of the most poignant scenes in all devotional writings, a scene we are not likely to forget, for the church has made it, along with Paul on the Damascus Road, a paradigm for the whole of Christendom.

Later, a mature Augustine mulled over Psalm 129, maybe recalling his own experience:

> For our depths is this mortal life. Whoever understands himself
> to be in the depths cries out, groans, sighs, until he is delivered
> from the depths, and comes to Him whose seat is above all
> depths. He is above the Cherubim, above all things He has cre-
> ated, not only bodily but spiritual things. Until the soul comes
> to Him; until His own image, that image which is man, and
> which in these depths has been tossed about by constant waves
> and worn away, becomes liberated by Him.[8]

Has Augustine here bequeathed to all Christendom a dogma, the
absolute pattern for conversion? Must the sinner sink so low in order to
testify to grace which raises him so high? Is it necessary to be utterly
wretched in order to become sublimely happy?

> Since we were not fit to grasp things eternal, and since we were
> weighed down by the foulness of sins, gathered on us by the
> love of temporal things, and as it were naturally implanted in us
> by the seed of mortality, it was neccessary that we should be
> cleansed. But cleansed we could not be, so as to be attuned to
> things eternal, except through things temporal, to which we
> were already attuned and by which we were held fast.[9]

Cassiciacum A.D. 386–387

It was natural that Augustine made an abrupt change in life style in
September. He was emotionally spent and time was needed for the
thoughtful relaxation which had been contemplated for months. "Besides this, during the summer I had developed a weakness of the lungs,
the result of too much study. I found breathing difficult and had pains
in the chest. . . . My voice was husky and I could not speak for a long
time." His popularity was dwindling; the Milanese were laughing at
his African accent. An important decision was made, he resigned his
post, "I notified the people of Milan that they must find another vendor
of words. . . . I wrote to . . . the saintly Ambrose . . . He told me to
read the prophet Isaiah."[10]

A beautiful spot had been located, an estate belonging to Verecundus, "his country house at Cassiciacum, where we found
rest . . . far from the world and its troubles." Verecundus originally
was not a Christian, but later professed his faith, died, and now Augustine is sure God is "repaying Verecundus with the contentment of your

paradise, where nothing ever fades away . . . in your mountain, your fruitful mountain."[11] Mountains were indeed in Augustine's thinking, for in the distance could be seen Mt. Rosa; a range of snow-covered Alpine peaks appeared on the far horizon, joining the Apennines to the south. Nearby was Lake Como. It was a majestic setting.

Cassiciacum was an old building, originally intended as a summer house; it had been occupied but part of the year. Over the years this comfortable structure had been renovated and enlarged. There were baths—which pleased Augustine's company—and they constituted the chief luxury. Frescoes probably adorned the walls, and there were doubtless mosaic floor patterns. There was a kitchen garden as well as grazing lands, meadows, and ploughed fields and a number of beautiful chestnut trees. As autumn wore on the leaves turned yellow and deep gold. Heaped by the roadside, they fell into the stream, choaking it into silence. Augustine always remembered the murmur of the water and the saffron leaves, almost blanketing the delightful sound.

Augustine now had his coterie of philosophers: Alypius, who had likewise resigned his position in Milan; Nebridius, who was still teaching but able to join the party from time to time. There were Augustine's cousins, Rusticus and Lastidianus, as well as the students Trygetius and Licentius, the son of Romanianus. Of course there was brother Navigius and Adeodatus, now almost a teenager. And the one who directed the entire household was Monica. It was a dream come true, a situation ideal for heart-to-heart sharing; an Order marked by discipline, rigorous study, and intense prayer, but with plenty of time for leisure under the vine-covered pergola.

Marriage, no matter how advantageous, was completely out of the question, for Augustine was free. He was free to rejoice in the Psalms, to pray for the coming of the Paraclete, and to wish the wretched Manichees might hear Truth: he hoped "they would have been made to feel the errors of their ways and would have disgorged it like vomit."[12] True, there had been the "agony of a toothache, and when the pain became so great that I could not speak, my heart prompted me to ask all my friends who were with me to pray to you for me." What was the nature of that pain? "Deep within me I recognized the working of your will and I praised your name, rejoicing in my faith."

Out of this brief holiday, from September to early February, came four significant works by Augustine. "I began at last to serve you with my pen," he joyously noted. "The books I wrote are evidence of this, although the old air can still be sensed in them." Writing became the agency for release, ideas, feelings. Cassiciacum is his final fling at assuming the role of neoclassical philosopher. It is likewise his concluding vacation. Never again—in the whole of a lifetime—would he enjoy such relaxed, unencumbered peace: majestic mountains, dark blue sky, deep green of the woodlands, the fragrance of mint and aniseed. "The tradition begun by Socrates under the plane-trees on the banks of the Ilissus, is ending with Augustin under the chestnuts of Cassiciacum."[13]

Against the Academics

Written in November of A.D. 386 and addressed to Romanianus, in three volumes, *Against the Academics* displays Augustine's lively, vivacious style. There is warmth as he tells of those joyful, personal relationships. Poor Romanianus' lawsuit has been a failure:

> Romanianus, it is a fact that knowledge but seldom grows into wisdom, and only for the few. This is due either to the manifold turmoils of this life, in which you present yourself as an outstanding example; or to a certain languor, sloth, or dullness of sluggish minds; or to despair of discovery . . . or to an error . . . namely, a false assurance of having already found the truth.

And Romanianus himself, his personality? Augustine chides him: "In you is concealed—a thunderbolt, so to speak—in those clouds of domestic affairs; it remains hidden from many persons . . . but it cannot escape the notice of your intimate friends."

Augustine has a remarkable compassion for the victorious enemy in the lawsuit: "We must admit that he has a certain mental adornment, or rather, the seed, as it were, of such adornment."[14]

It is the personal reference that glows brightest. Augustine describes the beauty of a November morning which "dawned so calm and clear that it seemed better suited for nothing else than for calming and clearing our minds." Eagerly "we arose from our beds earlier than usual." Another charming tableau depicts the one problem regarding these splendid debates, lack of oil for the lamps: "At this point I postponed the debate to another day, because the darkness was making it difficult to use the stylus and because I saw that an entirely new and important subject of discussion was arising."[15]

There are references to Romanianus' son Licentius, a discerning youth in whom Augustine took much interest—and a wealthy father is always happy to learn of his offspring, who "has already begun to apply himself to philosophy." (He later dabbled in poetry with a work on Pyramus and Thisbe).

It would be a mistake to assume the work is a dialogue on fascinating trivia. Augustine is concerned about the issues raised by the Academics: what of the soul and its liberation, the return of the soul to its origin? He speaks of low and lustful desires, subdued, and thus the soul is freed. He talks of the skepticism of the Academics, of the rational justification for a concept of Truth. Basic in the work is the search for a doctrine of Wisdom upon which a philosophy could be established.

Not all of Augustine's writing was on the book itself; he was busy corresponding. "I should not venture, even in jest, to criticize [the Academics]," he wrote to Hermogenians, "[their] influence has always weighed strongly with me." He continues, "Therefore . . . I have imitated them rather than attacked them. . . . If any untainted stream flows from the Platonic spring, it seems to me that in these times it is better for it to be guided through shady and thorny thickets, for the possession of the few, rather than allowed to wander through open spaces where cattle break through, and where it is impossible for it to be kept clear." He goes on:

> Therefore, since I so willingly trust your opinion of my books, and since I rely on you so completely, that for me there can be no defect in your prudence nor deceit in your friendship, I beg you to think over very carefully and write back to me whether you approve my conclusion at the end of Book Three, a conclusion which I regard with more misgivings than assurance.[16]

On the Happy Life

"It originated on the occasion of my birthday," noted Augustine with manifest delight, "and was consummated during a three day's conversation."[17] And the book was written with alacrity. It was the Ides of November:

> After a breakfast light enough not to impede our powers of thinking, I asked all those of us who, not only that day but every day, were living together to have a congenial session in the bathing quarters, a quiet place fitting for the season.[18]

Not only were the baths comfortable, but the steam was very beneficial for Augustine's lung condition. In dialogue, he wrote exuberantly, asking: What is a blissful life? It comes only from a mind, a personality, wherein the basic values—knowing and loving—are essentially one. "Considering that the voyage to the port of philosophy—from which, indeed, one enters the hinterland of the happy life—must be charted only by rational choice."

The third day, the morning mists having dispersed, promising a sunny afternoon. "So we decided to go down to the little meadow nearby. After we were all seated in what seemed a comfortable spot,"[19] the colloquy was resumed. And Plato's Academy in all its glory was not as brilliant as Augustine's seminar on the soft grass that November afternoon.

There are so many anecdotes of the friends, but especially of Monica, who holds absolute sway in the household, "in the first, our mother, to whose merits, in my opinion, I owe everything that I live." Augustine tells us, quite frankly, that he and Navigius did not always agree. It was a brother's prerogative, rather unlike the attitude of respectful—and sometimes docile—students. Navigius exercised the familiarity of a brother, and challenged Augustine, as in the discussion on food, "Navigius with his troublesome liver ought to be more cautious about sweets," chided Augustine. "Such food will surely cure me," responded the brother, "for the dish which you have set before us, mixed and spiced as it is, will, as Cicero says of Hymettic honey, bitterly sweet and will not bloat my stomach." They also teased Trygetius about his excessive appetite.

It was a salutary period for a man who had endured so much frustration and turmoil and *On the Happy Life* reflected the mood. Once the manuscript was completed Augustine put it aside and turned to another theme. A new book was in the offing.

On Order

Augustine wrote *On Order* in December, in answer to a poem by
Zenobius. He tells us of the order of life itself, and all order lies within
the framework of God's will: "I treated the important question of
whether the order of divine Providence embraces all things, the good
and the evil."[20] What prompted the writing?

At Cassiciacum, Augustine frequently suffered from insomnia. In
the dark bedroom he listened. There was the murmuring of the stream,
and he noticed the pauses in the sound. At that moment Licentius, who
shared the room, took his club and rapped on the floor to frighted
"some troublesome mice." It was now obvious that Trygetius was
likewise wide awake. It was a perfect opportunity for another discussion—on pauses in the flow of sound.[21] Was there an order, a secret
harmony in nature?

Later, as they made their way to the baths they came upon two
cocks fighting. Augustine immediately saw "a certain order . . . in all
the movements of these fowls deprived of reason." He noted how
proud the victor was, strutting and pluming himself, while the vanquished, now without voice and a neck plucked, was the very symbol
of shame.[22] These were topics in which Augustine reveled.

There is a description of morning prayer, prayers of great emotion
"with tears and anguish." Things great and small, just as clash of personalities, represent part of the ongoing of an orderly world.

Very loving terms are used about Monica:

> I know and can affirm without the slightest hesitation, Mother,
> that it is through your prayers that God has given me the
> thought of putting above all else the discovery of truth, of wish-
> ing, meditating, loving nothing besides. And I strongly believe
> that it is your prayer which will enable me to acquire this most
> wonderful good which your own merits have made me desire.[23]

It was during these months, he says, that he came to appreciate her intellectual qualities: "I realized that her mind was perfectly adapted to
true philosophy." He describes her utter shock at hearing Licentius,
"who had gone out for needs of nature," singing a psalm—in the la-
trine. Never! And the youth jestingly replied, "As if, should some enemy confine me here, God would not hear my voice!"

Augustine wrote to Zenobius at this time:

> We had agreed, I think, that none of the things which a bodily
> sense reveals to us can remain unchanged for even an instant,
> and that everything shifts, flows away, and has no hold on the
> present, which is to say, in Latin, that it has no being. The true
> and divine philosophy warns us to check and tame the love of
> such things, so dangerous and so full of penalties for us; and,
> while the body is engaged in its own activity, the mind should
> be carried away entirely enamored of what alone remains un-
> changed, of what is not a passing attraction for us wayfarers.[24]

On Order disclosed a certain decorousness which had now come to
Augustine, displacing the wild disarray he had so long experienced.
Not only was there orderly rhythm within the universe, there was order
in his own life.

Augustine's cloisterlike days were never languid. He was bom-
barded with ideas, and soon another book was underway as a fresh new
year was born.

Soliloquies

Augustine wrote the *Soliloquies* during the winter months, and this
self-portrait was "induced by my zeal and love for searching out, by
reason, the truth concerning those matters which I especially desired to
know ... questioning myself and answering myself."[25] And so:

> While I was turning over in my mind many and divers matters,
> searching ceaselessly and intently through many a day for my
> own self and my good, and what evil should be avoided, all at
> once a voice spoke to me.[26]

It is the sheer beauty of the devotional life which marks the work,
as in his opening prayer:

> God, through whom all things, which of themselves were not,
>   come to be.
> God, who has not permitted to perish even that which is
>   mutually destructive.
> God, who from nothing did create this world which the eyes of
>   all perceive to be most beautiful.
> God, who did not cause evil but caused it to become not most
>   evil.

> God, who to the few that flee for refuge to that which truly is, shows evil to be nothing.
> God, through whom the universe, even with those things which are sinister in it, is perfect.
> God, from whom dissonance to the extreme limit is nothing, since better things are brought in concert with the worse.
> God, who is loved knowingly or unknowingly by everything that is capable of loving.
> God, in whom are all things, yet to whom neither the vileness of any creature is vile, nor its error erroneous.

Augustine then pleads with Reason, how might he "with certainty" reach his goal:

> **A.** Why do you torment me; why do you probe so deeply; why do you go down so low? Now, I cannot restrain my tears any longer.
>
> **R.** Now, restrain your tears and control your feelings. You have certainly wept much and surely your weak chest supports this with difficulty.

Again:

> **A.** I give you thanks, and, when we are in silence, I will energetically and carefully go over these things with myself and you.
>
> **R.** Believe steadily in God and, as far as you can, entrust yourself wholly to Him. Do not choose to be, so to speak, your own master and under your own dominion, but proclaim yourself the servant of Him who is our kindest and most helpful Lord. For, if you do this, He will not cease to lift you up to Himself, and He will allow nothing to happen to you which is not for your good, even though you do not know it.
>
> **A.** I hear, I believe, and, as far as I am able, I obey; I pray very much to God Himself in order that I may accomplish very much. Or, do you want anything further of me?
>
> **R.** It is well enough for the time being. Later on, when you have beheld Him, you will do whatsoever He commands you.

Augustine sagely concludes, "I will never be convinced that we have asked God's help in vain." The conversation continues:

> **A.** One cannot sufficiently emphasize how much this evil is to be feared. What kind of eternal life will that be or what death

ought not to be preferred to it, if the soul so lives as we see it living in a newly born infant, not to speak of the life which goes on within the womb, for I do believe there is life there.

R. Be of good heart! As we already know, God will aid us in our quest, and, after this body He promises us what is most blessed, abounding in Truth, and free from all deception.

A. May it be as we hope!

Soliloquies deserves a place among the great devotional writings. Augustine was at his creative best:

O God, our Father, who does admonish us to pray, and who does grant us that which we ask of You, since in truth, when we pray to You, we live better and we are better: hear me, quivering in this darkness, and stretch forth Your right hand to me. Send forth Your light to me, call me back from my wanderings, and may I by Your guidance return to myself and to You. Amen.[27]

It is singularly appropriate that *Soliloquies* concludes Augustine's writings at Cassiciacum. He closes the period on a note of praise to God. Here was his mainstay: faith. He had come a long way. From the morass of sin and perdition he had scaled the alpine heights of prayer. It was his paean of gratitude to the God who had forgiven him, upheld him, guided him.

Cassiciacum betokens a tranquil interlude in Augustine's life. With closest friends and family he lived, wrote, thought, and prayed—amid charming surroundings. Peace had come. Rejected now were thoughts of marriage. With a measure of certainty he planned a future of quiet monastic life. The fellowship would continue to pursue attainment in philosophy, for they were quite proud and confident; they had merged Plato and Aristotle with John and Paul. It was exhilarating!

Now this blissful experiment would change; they must return to Milan. Lent was at hand. Augustine, Adeodatus, and Alypius had a never-to-be-forgotten spring before them. Ambrose was waiting at the baptistry:

When the time came for me to hand in my name for baptism, we left the country and went back to Milan. It was Alypius's wish to be reborn in you at the same time. He was already endued with the humility which fits a man for your sacraments, and he had subjected his body to such stern discipline that he would even walk barefoot on the icy soil of Italy, a thing few would venture to do. With us we took the boy Adeodatus, my natural son born of my sin.[28]

Preparation

Once back in Milan, during the weeks prior to baptism, Augustine continued his far-reaching personal readjustment: drawing to the Church, moving from classical philosophy to a Christocentric theology. It is his torrential spiritual springtime. Augustine instinctively put his thoughts on paper, enabling us to see firsthand the remarkable evolution. What were his thoughts?

Augustine invited Adeodatus to join in projecting a new volume, "whose title is *On the Teacher.* In this, there is a discussion, an investigation, and the discovery that there is no teacher who teaches man knowledge except God, according to what, in truth, is written in the Gospel: 'One is your Master, the Christ.' "[29] It "consists of a dialogue between Adeodatus and myself. You know that all the ideas expressed by the second speaker in the discussions are his." With glowing enthusiasm the father adds, "although he was only sixteen when it took place." The youth had remarkable talent, "his intelligence left me spell-bound." There is no question as to bond between father and son. Adeodatus was so like his father in spirit and mind. "I remember him without apprehension," said Augustine, "for there was nothing in his childhood or youth or in any part of his life which need make me fear for him."[30]

Their joint venture, *On the Teacher,* follows Socratic dialogue. Augustine sets forth his view of Christian culture vs. the old paganism.

> **A.** What would you say we are trying to do whenever we speak?
>
> **Ad.** As it strikes me right now, we want either to teach or learn.[31]

And thus Adeodatus is given instruction in various principles. An example would be a discussion of "names signifying bodily objects"—

A. Are we going to call color a body? Do we not rather speak of it as a quality of bodies?

Ad. That is right.

A. Here again, why can it not be indicated with the finger? Or do you also include with bodies the qualities of bodies, so that these, as well as bodies, can be shown without words, whenever they are present?

Ad. When I said "bodies," I intended that all things corporeal should be understood, namely, everything which the senses perceive in bodies.

A. But consider whether even here you should allow for exceptions.

Ad. That is sound advice. For I should not have said all things corporeal, but all things visible. I indeed acknowledge that through sound, odor, taste, weight, heat, and other qualities pertaining to the senses other than sight, cannot be perceived apart from bodies, and are therefore corporeal.[32]

Augustine clearly indicates his own insight on teaching:

Do teachers ever claim that it is their own thoughts that are grasped and retained, rather than the branches of learning themselves which they purport to transmit by their speaking? What . . . could ever prompt a man to send his child to school in order to have him learn what the teacher thinks? But when teachers have made use of words to explain all those branches of learning . . . then those who are known as pupils reflect within themselves whether what has been said is true, contemplating, that is, that inner truth according to their capacity.

On the Teacher is a gift to posterity, jointly composed by a father and son, neither of whom would have progeny to survive them.

A fresh addition was made to the African fellowship in Milan, "a young man from our own town, named Evodius. . . . He had been converted and baptized before us."[33] Augustine owed a tremendous debt to his African compatriots. They gave moral backing and inspiration— when he needed it most. It was during this lush springtime that yet another book was undertaken, "I wrote a book, *On the Immortality of the Soul*." Alas, "because of the intricacy and brevity of its reasoning, it is so obscure that even my attention flags as I read it and I, myself, can scarcely understand it."[34] Even so, he wrestles with the question he had earlier asked, "First of all I should like to know if I am immortal."[35]

Augustine established that the soul, because it knows the certainty of its own faculty for reasoning, must exist, "If we who reason exist, that is, if our mind does, and if correct reasoning without science is impossible—and only a mind in which science does not exist can be without science—then science exists in the mind of man."[36] He goes on to say:

> whatever exists and is immutable must necessarily exist always. On the other hand nobody denies that science exists. And whoever asserts that only the straight line drawn through the center of a circle is longer than any other line not drawn through the center, and that this statement belongs in the realm of science, as much as admits that there is an immutable science. Nothing in which something else exists always, cannot be but always. Nothing, however, that always is ever suffers the loss from itself of that in which it always exists.

And then he sums it up:

> When we reason, it is an act of our mind; for only that reason which understands, can reason. Neither the body understands . . . when the mind wishes to understand, it is turned away from the body. . . . All that the mind knows it possesses within itself. The human mind, therefore, lives always.[37]

One can almost hear Plotinus speaking. "The human body . . . is subject to change, and reason is immutable . . . all is subject to change that does not exist always in the same way . . . two and four make six . . . it is always true. . . . Such reasoning is not subject to change; therefore reason exists."[38]

Augustine goes to great length to speak of change, "let us see to what extent we are able to accept a change of the mind . . . in how many ways that which is called a change of the mind may be accepted . . . the mind is changed . . . according to the passions of the body, by age, sickness, pain, work, injury, and carnal desire; according to its own passions, in turn, through desire, joy, fear, worry, zeal, and study." He speaks of the human makeup, "the mind, which evidently surpasses the body. . . . Thus the mind's immortality is immediately proved, in case it can exist through itself . . . that which has this quality is by necessity incorruptible and, therefore, cannot perish.''[39]

Augustine concludes, ''The soul is more powerful and excellent than the body . . . since the body subsists by the soul . . . the soul itself can in no way be transformed into a body. For no body is made unless it receives its form from the soul. The soul . . . is present . . . not only in the entire mass of its body, but also in each of its individual parts. For it is the entire soul that feels the pain of a part of the body, yet it does not feel it in the entire body.''[40] *On the Immortality of the Soul* cogently reflects Greek thought. Plato would have been proud of his African-Christian disciple.

Spring of 387 also saw Augustine begin *On Music,* not to be completed until 391 in Africa. It was part of a projected cycle on liberal arts. ''I wrote six books *On Music.* The sixth of these became especially well known because in it a subject worthy of investigation was considered, namely, how, from corporeal and spiritual but changeable numbers, one comes to the knowledge of unchangeable numbers which are already in unchangeable truth itself.''[41]

Augustine begins with definitions, rhythm and meter:

> Music is the science of moving well. But that is because whatever moves and keeps harmoniously the measuring of time and intervals can already be said to move well. For it is already pleasing, and for this reason is already properly called mensuration. Yet it is possible for this harmony and measuring to please when they shouldn't. For example, if one should sing sweetly and dance gracefully, wishing thereby to be happy when the occasion demanded gravity, such a person would in no way be using harmonious mensuration well. In other words, that person uses ill or improperly the motion at one time called good because of its harmony.[42]

As though Augustine himself has become weary, ''We have delayed long enough, and very childishly, too. . . . For we only thought it ought to be undertaken so adolescents, or men of any age God has endowed with a good natural capacity, might with reason guiding be torn away, not quickly but gradually, from the fleshly senses and letters it is difficult for them not to stick to, and adhere with the love of unchangeable truth to one God and Master of all things who with no mean term whatever directs human minds.''[43]

On Music reveals spiritual progress and yet a tremendous indebtedness to a rich, though pagan, past. He delights in philosophy, but he has found Christ:

> I in my littleness have gathered with you what I could and as I could on such great matters. But, if any read this talk of ours committed to writing, they must know these things have been written by persons much weaker than those who, having followed the authority of the two Testaments, by believing, hoping, and loving, venerate and worship the consubstantial and unchangeable Trinity of the one highest God from whom, through whom, and in whom are all things. For they are purified, not by flashing human reasoning, but by the effective and burning fire of charity.[44]

And these concluding lines indeed reflect an older, more established man of the Church.

Baptism A.D. 387

Ash Wednesday, March 10, ushered in the most important Lent of Augustine's life: instruction from Ambrose. These daily lessons would have been received with alacrity. With the arrival of Holy Week, Augustine's heart beat faster. On Maundy Thursday, April 22, in the presence of the congregation, he recited the Creed, and on that night refrained from bathing and began a strict fast.

Holy Saturday found Augustine returning to the basilica along with all *competentes*—those requesting baptism. Ambrose laid hands upon him, exorcising any demons. Thus purged, Augustine and the others knelt before Ambrose and, facing the East made three solemn promises of obedience to God's Law. Ambrose then breathed upon him, making the sign of the cross on his forehead, lips and breast. Paschal Vigil followed, certain psalms were read, "As the hart longs for flowing streams, so longs my soul for you, O God," and Augustine listened, "my tears have been my food day and night. . . Why are you cast down, O my soul, and why are you disquieted within me? Hope in God; for I shall again praise him, my help and my God."

Once more Augustine faced the East, vowing thrice to reject Satan, renounce his work, his pomp. "Do you believe in God the Father Almighty; in Jesus Christ the Son of God; in the Holy Spirit? asked Ambrose, and Augustine solemnly responded, "I do believe." Instilled within him was the awesomeness of the responsibility about to be undertaken. Christian mysteries, such as the Lord's Prayer, were not freely made known to unbelievers. Augustine listened to forbidding warnings against polytheism and idolatry. He heard, with special attentiveness, explanation of the doctrine of the Incarnation; there were also repeated warnings of ghastly personal retribution after death for the unfaithful.

It was now Easter Eve, and the moment had arrived. In the baptistry, alone, Augustine came from behind curtains, completely naked. Divestiture of clothing represented total rejection of all worldliness—women even removed hairpins. A supplicant's body was to be throughly cleansed of the filth of past sins. Three times Ambrose would have held Augustine's shoulders beneath the flowing water—in the name of the Trinity. "Let it say to its Lord: Holy, holy, holy, Lord, my God, it is in your name that we are baptized, Father, Son, and Holy Spirit, and it is in your name that we baptize, Father, Son, and Holy Spirit, because among us too, in Christ his Son, God has made a heaven and earth, the members of his Church, spiritual and carnal."[45]

When Augustine emerged from the pool, a priest would have anointed him with oil mixed with balsam. Ambrose made the Cross on his forehead, and, observing a practice established in Milan, knelt and washed Augustine's feet. Dressed in a tunic of pure white wool, the baptized Augustine joined others in the enormous basilica, now glorious in the light of hundreds of candles, and, standing by the altar, would have participated in the mysteries of the Risen Christ: amid the dawning glory of the morning Easter sun, mass and Holy Communion. He would then have been given a drink of milk and honey, as a citizen of that new kingdom, untrodden Canaan. Easter Sunday, April 25, 387 would ever remain a high and holy day in Augustine's memory.

Years later, Augustine composed his poem—the only one he ever wrote—in praise of the Paschal Candle. He had never forgotten that moment of physical and spiritual brilliance:

>   These are your gifts; they are good, for you in your goodness
>   have made them.
>   Nothing in them is from us, save for sin when, neglectful
>   of order,
>   We fix our love on the creature, instead of on you,
>   the Creator.[46]

Baptism would forever hold particular meaning for Augustine; it
was a symbol of new birth:

>   He who produces or worships any symbol, unaware of what it
>   means, is enslaved to a sign. On the other hand, he who either
>   uses or esteems a beneficial sign, divinely established, whose
>   efficacy and meaning he knows, does not worship this visible
>   and transitory sign; he worships that reality. . . . Examples of
>   these are the sacraments of Baptism and the celebration of the
>   Body and Blood of the Lord. When anyone who has been in-
>   structed observes these practices, he understands to what they
>   refer, so that he does not venerate them in carnal slavery, but
>   rather in spiritual liberty.[47]

Augustine experienced fulfillment of his most cherished hope. "We
were baptized, and all anxiety over the past melted away from us. The
days were too short . . . tears flowed from me when I heard your hymns
and canticles, for the sweet singing of your Church moved me deeply
. . . my feelings of devotion overflowed, so that the tears streamed
down. But they were tears of gladness."[48]

Baptism continued to be stressed in Augustine's writings. "By the
work of your saints, O God, your sacraments have moved amidst the
flood of the world's temptations to bathe its peoples in the waters of
your baptism and imprint your name upon them." In speaking of living
creatures dwelling on dry land and in the sea, he makes the analogy:
"This is because the earth no longer needs baptism as it did when it
was covered by the waters and as the heathen need it still; for ever
since you ordained that we should enter heaven through baptism there
has been no other way to come into the Kingdom."[49]

During the weeks following baptism, Augustine maintained an interesting yet somewhat mystifying relationship with Ambrose and his
church. Ambrose was always "our bishop" and the "practice of singing hymns, in which the faithful united fervently with heart and

voice,"[50] was dear to Augustine. Is it possible that the two men ever became close? Augustine was intrigued by the discovery in 386—at a most opportune time in Ambrose's career—of the bodies of twin martyrs. The church needed unification and strengthening.

> A miracle that happened at Milan while I was there, when a blind man had his sight restored, succeeded in becoming more widely known because Milan is an important city, and because the emperor was there at the time. A great crowd had gathered to see the bodies of the martyrs Protasius and Gervasius, and the miracle took place before all those witnesses. Those bodies had been lost and nothing at all was known about them; but their hiding-place was revealed in a dream to Ambrose, bishop of Milan, and they were discovered.[51]

Ambrose knew how to take advantage of every situation. "After the bodies had been discovered and dug up, they were carried to Ambrose's basilica with the honor that was due to them."[52] And Augustine understood!

Second only to Monica was Ambrose in influence upon Augustine: preaching, suggested readings, baptism and instruction in the life of faith, yet there was distance:

> The one thing which afflicts me is that I cannot make known to Ambrose, as I would like, my love for him or for truth. Doubtless he would take pity on my thirst for truth, and quench it more quickly than he thinks. This is because he has security, being absolutely convinced of the immorality of the soul, and he does not know that there may be men who have realized the misery of their ignorance and whom it [would] be cruel not to help, especially when they ask for assistance.[53]

Life was falling into focus. "Everyone," said Augustine, "converted to God, will find that while his delights and pleasures have been changed, they have not been taken away." It was time to leave Italy—work in Milan was over—for Africa was calling her son to come home, that inward compulsion which cannot be resisted. He was now experiencing a new existence; he was a new creation, and this may have been in the back of his mind as he later wrote: "He liberates us in all things; and to serve him is the most profitable thing for all; and to please in his service is the one and perfect liberation."[54]

Ostia and the Death of Monica A.D. 387

Monica was in wretched health; possibly it was the determinant for an immediate return to Africa. Ominous news had also come; the brutal Maximus, the usurper, was about to invade Italy—tantamount to civil war. This would have closed all Italian ports. Whatever the reason, Augustine and party took leave of Milan.

Civil war struck just as Augustine reached Ostia. Sailing for Carthage was impossible, hence requiring a stay in the port city. Possibly they lived with the Anicii,[55] the wealthiest family in the empire, and Ambrose would have provided the introduction. Here they made a temporary home during the autumn of 387 as Maximus' armies marched into Italy.

It must have been a spacious house where Augustine and Monica shared the last days and final hours of her life. Augustine provides the tableaux—done in retrospect and highly colored, for it is a son describing his mother—and he reaches heights of artistry. They were resting after the long journey from Rome, and anticipating the voyage to Africa. "My mother and I were alone, leaning from a window which overlooked the garden in the courtyard of the house where we were staying at Ostia. We were waiting there . . . we were talking alone together and our conversation was serene and joyful."[56]

Augustine speaks to us as though we were in the room with him. "Our conversation led us to the conclusion that no bodily pleasure, however great it might be and whatever earthly light might shed lustre upon it, was worthy of comparison, or even of mention, beside the happiness of the life of the saints." Their thoughts "ranged over the compass of material things. . . . Higher still we climbed . . . we came to our own souls and passed beyond . . . to that place of everlasting plenty . . . the food of truth. There life is that Wisdom by which all these things that we know are made, all things that ever have been and all that are yet to be. . . . And while we spoke of the eternal Wisdom, longing for it and straining for it with all the strength of our hearts, for one fleeting instant we reached out and touched it."

Augustine's narrative reaches sublime heights: "Suppose . . . that the tumult of a man's flesh were to cease and all that his thoughts can conceive . . . were silent . . . passing beyond; . . . suppose that his dreams and the visions of his imagination spoke no more . . . and their message is this: We did not make ourselves, but he who abides for ever made us. Suppose . . . he alone should speak to us . . . suppose that this state were to continue . . . would not this be what we are to understand by the words *Come and share the joy of your Lord?*" [57]

It was a moment of ethereal sensitivity: "the world, for all its pleasures, seemed a paltry place compared with the life we spoke of." Monica told her son that her one reason for living "was to see you a Catholic Christian before I died." God had fulfilled her request. "What is left for me to do in this world?" Her mission now consummated, she was at peace. "I scarcely remember what answer I gave."

"It was about five days after this . . . that she took to her bed with a fever." She lost consciousness for a time, and on recovery asked, "Where was I?" She then gave simple, clear instructions: "You will bury your mother here." What? Not in Africa? It seemed impossible. Augustine attempted to keep back the tears. "My brother said something to the effect that he wished for her sake that she would die in her own country." In answering, Monica gives her majestic testimony, "See how he talks!" She continued: "It does not matter where you bury my body. Do not let that worry you! All I ask of you is that, wherever you may be, you should remember me at the altar of the Lord." She fell silent. Augustine mused, "How little the human mind can understand God's purpose!" He remembered an observation of hers about the place of burial; "Nothing is far from God . . . and I need have no fear that he will not know where to find me when he comes to raise me to life at the end of the world." This declaration takes on increased meaning in light of Augustine's recollection. "I had always known, and well remembered now, my mother's great anxiety to be buried beside her husband's body in the grave which she had provided and prepared for herself. Because they had lived in the greatest harmony, she had always wanted this extra happiness. She had wanted it to be said of them that, after her journeyings across the sea, it had been granted to her that the earthly remains of husband and wife should be joined as one and covered by the same earth." [58]

Were Augustine's parents really that happy throughout their marriage? Time heals old wounds and we tend to remember joyous experiences. Augustine continues: "And so on the ninth day of her illness, when she was fifty-six and I thirty-three, her pious and devoted soul was set free from the body." He writes of the swell of emotion that came over him. "I closed her eyes, and a great wave of sorrow surged into my heart. It would have overflowed in tears if I had not made a strong effort of the will and stemmed the flow, so that the tears dried in my eyes."

Adeodatus gave vent to real emotion "and only ceased his cries when we all checked him." In reality Augustine "wanted to cry like a child" but an inner voice would not permit it. "Weeping and moaning" did not seem appropriate, for "such lamentations are the usual accompaniment of death when it is thought of as a state of misery or as total extinction." Certainly, this was the *usual* concept of death.

"What was it, then, that caused me such deep sorrow?" The "wound was fresh" and the life shared by Monica and Augustine that had been "so precious and so dear . . . was suddenly cut off." He found comfort in memory: "I did what I could for my mother in the last stages of her illness, she had caressed me and said that I was a good son to her. With great emotion she told me that she could not remember ever having heard me speak a single hard or disrespectful word against her."

Adeodatus was now calm; the entire household sang Psalm 101, "I will sing of loyalty and justice." Others came to join them. In another room, Augustine rather dispassionately discussed, "without irreverence," various "matters suitable to the occasion." Those whose duty it was "made arrangements for the funeral," and all the while Augustine was writhing "O Lord, how I suffered," but the friends knew it not. They "thought I had no sense of grief." Outwardly he held up, appeared poised, but inwardly "I was stifling in my heart."

The same remarkable composure continued as "the body was carried out for burial, I went and returned without a tear. I did not weep even during the prayers which we recited while the sacrifice of our redemption was offered for my mother and her body rested by the grave before it was laid in the earth, as is the custom there." Did he have this service in mind when he later wrote, "If an expensive funeral is of any advantage to an evil man, a cheap one, or none at all, is of no disadvantage to a devout soul," and "a large gathering of the household put on a great show."[59]

Augustine prayed God would "heal my sorrow, but you did not grant my prayer." He decided he "would go to the baths," hoping to relax, for "bathing rids the mind of anxiety." Alas, it provided little solace; "water could not wash away the bitter grief from my heart." Rest, a bit of sleep, brought some assuagement. While in bed, Augustine reflected on the lines of Psalm 68, as arranged by Ambrose, possibly Monica's favorite hymn: could it have been used at the funeral?

> Maker of all things! God most high!
> Great Ruler of the starry sky!
> Who, robing day with beauteous light,
> [Has] clothed in soft repose the night.
>
> That sleep may wearied limbs restore,
> And fit for toil and use once more;
> May gently sooth the careworn breast,
> And lull our anxious griefs to rest.[60]

At last release came through tears "which I had been holding back streamed down, and I let them flow as freely as they would, making of them a pillow for my heart."

Augustine made a poignant request of his readers: "And now, O Lord, I make you my confession in this book. Let any man read it who will. Let him understand it as he will. And if he finds that I sinned by weeping for my mother, . . . let him not mock at me. For this was the mother, . . . who had wept over me for many years. . . . Let him not mock at me but weep himself. . . . Let him weep for my sins to you."

Does Augustine over-dramatize his mother? Is he the little boy who clutches her apron strings, even after she is dead? This much we can affirm: the relationship was intensely human, reflecting some of the deepest emotions of life, not superficial nor artificial.

> Let her rest with her husband. He was her first husband and she married no other after him—inspire those who read this book to remember Monica, your servant, at your altar and with her Pa-

tricius, her husband, who died before her, by whose bodies you brought me into this life, though how it was I do not know.

He told her final wish: "the last request that my mother made to me shall be granted in the prayers of the many who read my confessions more fully than in mine alone."[61]

During the Cassiciacum days he had said, "Thanks to diligent observation during our life in common, I had already remarked her natural gifts and her ardent love of divine things."[62] Was Monica a paragon? Was she this scintillating? It is doubtful. What we have is a son's loving report on the simple yet wise observations of his mother. "If one wishes for and possesses good things, he is happy," she once commented, "but if he wishes for evil things, even though he has them, he is unhappy." To which an admiring and radiant Augustine fulsomely responded, "You have truly reached the citadel of philosophy, Mother."[63]

In the long list of famous men who have paid excessive tribute to their mothers, few have surpassed Augustine. His love placed her on a pedestal and possibly gave her far more credit than she deserved, but, "If I have not perished in error and evil, it is because of the tears, the long and faithful tears of my mother."[64]

Was Augustine endeavoring to be objective as he wrote of Monica? Of course not! In the final analysis, can one be objective about one's own mother?

Italy A.D. 388

Augustine sadly trudged from Ostia back to Rome during the early months of 388. Ports continued to be closed; there could be no immediate return to Carthage. He would fill the time writing in the City of the Caesars. "I wrote," he recorded, "a dialogue in which there is a lengthy treatment and discussion of the soul."[65] It was a "careful and searching examination" substantiating the view that while the soul lacks a tangible quality, it is a *tremendous* reality. It is a dialogue with Evodius. "I see that you have plenty of time on your hands; please tell me how you would answer some foolish questions of mine which, I believe, are not foolish or out of order," asked Evodius. "State briefly what you want to hear about the soul," replied Augustine. Thus *On the*

Magnitude of the Soul begins, discussing the origin, nature, extent, union with the body, nature of this union, and then—in conclusion—the character of the soul as separated from the physical.

As illustration, Augustine makes use of geometric designs, "I call a figure that in which any space is enclosed by a line or lines." He draws circles, triangles, rectangles, "How many angles in this figure?" Again he asks, "Are all the lines equal?"[66] All things are resolved in the Etenal:

> God, therefore, supreme and true, by an inviolable and un-changing law by which He rules all creation, subjects the body to the soul, the soul to Himself, and so everything to Himself. In no act does God abandon the soul either for punishment or reward. For He has judged it to be the most beautiful, so that it is the exemplar of all reality, and all reality is so arranged in a hierarchy that anyone who considers the totality of things may not be offended by the lack of conformity in any part, and that every punishment and every reward of the soul should contribute something corresponding to the measured beauty and ar-rangement of all things.[67]

It was a masterful undertaking.

Augustine also completed book one of *On Free Will.* "While we were still staying in Rome, we wanted, by means of discussion, to in-quire into the source of evil, and we so conducted our disputation that we hoped that, if possible, considered and prolonged reasoning would bring to our understanding what we, on divine authority, believed about this matter, so far as we, with God's help, could accomplish our purpose through examination and discussion." He goes on: "We agree that the sole source of evil is the free choice of the will."[68]

A major point: "God is to be praised. In fact, this discussion was taken up because of those who deny that the source of evil has its origin in the free choice of the will and who contend that, if this is so, God, the Creator of all natures, is to be blamed." Of course, he is speaking of the Manichees who "wish to introduce a kind of fundamental or nat-ural evil, unchangeable and coeternal with God."

In addition, Augustine wrote two companion pieces: *On the Morals of the Catholic Church* and *On the Morals of the Manichaeans,* He wrote: "After my baptism but while I was in Rome, unable to endure in silence the boasting of the Manichaeans about their false and fallacious continence or abstinence because of which, in order to deceive the unlearned, they consider themselves superior to true Christians."[69] He was now a Catholic, and he took up the cudgel with all the vigor of the recent convert. New life was before him.

> The root is living, but in winter time the vigorous tree looks just like a withered one. For in winter time, both the tree which is vigorous and which is withered, are both bare of the beauty of the leaves, both are empty of the adornment of fruit. Summer will come, and there will be a distinction between the trees. The living root puts forth leaves and is pregnant with fruit; the withered one will remain as barren in the heat of summer as if it was winter . . . So our summer is the coming of Christ.[70]

A spiritual summer would soon be at hand.

Augustine was impatient to return to Africa where he, now sure of his vocational plans, would serve God and man through the Church. His service would be in the dedicated capacity of a layman. He and his fellows would be *Servants of God*, committed to a contemplative ministry, and he knew just the place for such a monastery: the small family estate at Tagaste which had been bequeathed to him by his parents. It was the last parcel of land he would ever own. He would give it away. He was so eager to go home! He had never really gotten the desert sand out of his shoes.

VIII

At Home in Africa

Return to Carthage A.D. 388

In late 388 Augustine's party finally arrived in Carthage. He was at last home in the Mother Country. Upon his arrival in Carthage, Augustine tells of the miraculous "healing" which took place in the home of his noted and gracious host, Innocentius. It is a choice story. "I was present as an eyewitness; for when I came with my brother Alypius from overseas, when we were not yet ordained though already servants of God, Innocentius entertained us, we were staying in his house at the time." Few people in Carthage—quite understandably—knew of the incident.

Innocentius, an important lawyer and devout churchman, "sometime counsellor of the vice-prefecture," suffered from "fistulas, having a number of them intertwined in the rectum, and others more deep-seated." Surgeons had operated and prescribed treatment—all acutely painful. One ulcer failed to heal, and when one medical man suggested additional surgery, Innocentius "angrily dismissed him from the house." There was delay and the patient grew "extremely apprehensive" and burst out, "Are you going to operate again?" A new doctor was called in and after considerable time announced the same verdict: the knife. "The patient was aghast; he turned deadly pale," and the house was filled with lamentations, such wild grief "that it resembled the mourning at a funeral." All the clergy, including Bishop Aurelius, Saturninus the bishop of Uzalis, Gulosus a presbyter, and Augustine "betook ourselves to prayers" when the unfortunate Innocentius insisted upon it, likewise imploring them to be present the following morning for the shuddersome scene, for he knew he was going to die.

"The dreadful morning" the "servants of God" arrived as promised, and they did their best to raise the patient's "drooping spirits." His body "was being laid in position" and "bandages were untied; the place was bared" and the dread instruments glittered in the surgeon's hand. When the physician extended his hand to the shivering Innocentius—lying prostrate upon his stomach—ready to make the incision, he examined in every way. The doctor "found it firmly cicatrized." It was a miracle! Healing.

Said Augustine, the "rejoicing that followed, the thanksgiving to God . . . I have not words to express. The scene can be better imagined than described."[1] And we can almost see the wry smile, the impish gleam in Augustine's eye as he tells the story—some thirty years later.

Tagaste A.D. 388–391

Once established in Tagaste, the goodly fellowship of Christian philosophers hoped to pause for an interim of quietude. Augustine wrote Nebridius back in Carthage: "I cannot taste and relish that true good unless a certain measure of carefree leisure falls to my lot. Believe me, a man does not achieve freedom from fear through his own insensibility, or boldness, or greed of empty glory, or superstitious credulity, but only by a considerable detachment from perishable things."[2] Much thinking and lofty writing—but this idyllic situation endured for a very short time. Two blows shattered the tranquility. First there was news of the death of Nebridius.

There had been such a lively correspondence between the two intimate friends. "Your letters are as precious to me as my eyes," wrote Nebridius. "For they are great, not in length, but in the subjects. . . . They speak to me of Christ, of Plato, of Plotinus."[3] Nebridius begged Augustine to come to Carthage. Augustine declined, but reciprocated with an invitation for his dear friend to journey to Tagaste, for "we can live here more satisfactorily than at Carthage or even in the country." He went on that it was impossible to make the trips to Carthage, he could not "go backward and forward frequently, so as to be now with you and now with them." "To both groups, however," he went on, "it is possible to be sanctified in peaceful quiet."[4] Nebridius replied that he was ill and could not make the journey, tiresome as it was. Augustine debated whether or not he should visit his friend and decided against it—he bitterly disliked travel. He was all the more grief-stricken when he learned of Nebridius'passing. Why had he not gone? Why had he not endured the inconvenience of travel? It was an unspeakable loss.

Perhaps the most crushing blow to Augustine was the death of that precocious gift from God. Adeodatus had blessed his father beyond measure:

> But you took him from this world early in life, and now I remember him without apprehension. . . . We made him our companion, in your grace no younger than ourselves. Together we were ready to begin our schooling in your ways. We were baptized, and all anxiety over the past melted away from us. The days were all too short, for I was lost in wonder and joy, meditating upon your far-reaching providence for the salvation of the human race.[5]

Now, just eighteen, the prodigy was dead. Augustine's family had slipped away. True, there was Navigius, but the tie between the brothers was never strong. They had all gone: Patricius, the common-law-wife, Monica, Nebridius, and now Adeodatus. His family was no more and his heart was broken. No longer could this, or any retreat, be regarded solely for deliberation and reflection. "That, indeed, is something—to be stripped of vain cares and clothed with useful ones. But, I doubt whether any security is to be hoped for in this world."[6] Was it personal sorrow that brought matters into focus? He would establish a real monastery. His Tagaste experiment was really a philosopher's retreat; now he would move into the heart of the church. His tie thus far was very strong, far more so than ever in Milan. Now it would be increased. The chief aim would be, not Plato and the like, but study of Scripture. Still, he would remain a layman. In fact, he avoided visiting towns where it was known that a priest was needed, lest he be taken by force—it frequently happened. Little did he know what was just before him.

It was during the Tagaste sojourn, in 390, that Augustine wrote *On*

True Religion, dedicating it to Romanianus: "I have written something on the Catholic religion, within the limits of what the Lord has granted me to do."[7] He was veritably moving into the vortex of Catholic life and faith. "At this time also I wrote a book . . . in which I argued repeatedly and lengthily that the one true God—that is, the Trinity, the Father, Son and Holy Spirit—is to be worshipped by the true religion, declaring also the greatness of that mercy of His through which, by a temporal dispensation, the Christian religion, which is the true religion, has been given to man; and it is man's obligation to be inclined, by a kind of delight, to this same worship of God."[8] There is little surprise that *On True Religion* is directed chiefly against the Manichees.

We behold the full metamorphosis in Augustine's thought: he is ardently Catholic, "The way of the good and blessed life is to be found entirely in the true religion . . . one God . . . worshipped and acknowledged."[9] Indeed, Christ has achieved gloriously that which Plato was never able to accomplish. It is à précis of Augustine's theology at the point in time of his return to Africa.

> If Plato and the rest of them, in whose names men glory, were to come to life again and find the churches full and the temples empty, and that the human race was being called away from desire for temporal and transient goods to spiritual and intelligible goods and to the hope of eternal life, and was actually giving its attention to these things, they would perhaps say . . . That is what we did not dare to preach to the people. We preferred to yield to popular custom rather than to bring the people over to our way of thinking and living.[10]

They had done their work well, those who had aided Augustine in his search for Truth. But of all, Augustine himself had toiled assiduously to learn, grow, become. Now he could say from his heart and soul, "The very Virtue and changeless Wisdom of God, consubstantial and coeternal with the Father, for our salvation deigned, in the temporal dispensation, to take upon himself our nature in order to teach us that men must worship what every rational intellectual creature must also worship."[11] Augustine the intellectual was speaking. His conversion was manifestly complete, yet he still regarded himself as one who would live out his years amid quiet, dignified surroundings, brooding over unfinished manuscripts. It would be a thoroughly Christian envi-

ronment and the endeavor unreservedly committed to Christlike aims
and ideals. Nonetheless, it would still savor of the philosopher at work.
An aggressive, evangelistic note was yet to be sounded. In the near future an unparalleled situation would present itself and the new note in
Augustine's voice would be heard—clearly.

Hippo Regius A.D. 391–395

In many respects, Augustine's life is best understood as a series of
quests. He was perpetually moving on to new concepts or to challenging situations in vocation, residence or thought. A favorite phrase was,
"What is the meaning of 'Seek His face evermore'?" He asks:

> Did the Psalmist mean by "evermore" the whole of the life we
> live here, whence we become conscious that we ought thus to
> seek, since even when found He is still to be sought? True,
> faith has already found Him, but hope still seeks Him. . . . Or
> when we shall have seen Him face to face as He is, will He still
> have to be sought, and to be sought for evermore because to be
> loved evermore?

Augustine believed "that finding should not end that seeking by which
love is testified, but with the increase of love the seeking of the found
One should increase."[12] So he continued his pilgrimage.

Ostensibly, Augustine journeyed to Hippo Regius to persuade a
wealthy clerk of the Imperial Ministry of the Interior to become a
monk. Hippo was an important African city, second only to Carthage;
here Augustine kept his rendezvous with destiny.

"I came as a young man to this city, as many of you know. I was
looking for a place to set up a monastery, to live with my 'brethren.' I
had given up all hope in this world."[13] He could not have made his
appearance at a more opportune time. The church was crying for
clergy, especially men who had capacity for leadership. Aging Bishop
Valerius, a Greek who spoke Latin with painful difficulty, was preaching in his Basilica of Peace. It was early in the year 391. In this particular service the bishop was lamenting the paucity of priests. Someone in
that congregation saw Augustine standing in the nave. Immediately the
cry was raised, "It is Augustine!" Pandemonium ensued. Willy-nilly

he was seized and pushed forward, the congregation by this time was in a frenzy, crying "Augustine a priest."

This bewildering practice was common in the African Church. Priests and bishops were frequently thus chosen by popular acclaim. Augustine would have been known as a proficient public speaker, and his books were now circulated. The Catholic population was weary of old Valerius' labored utterances; they wanted sermons in fresh language; yet more, they needed youthful leadership. Need for bishops was well known to Augustine. "I felt secure," he said, "for the place already had a bishop. I was grabbed. I was made a priest . . . and from there, I became your bishop."[14] At the moment, however, the crowd was insisting on the priesthood, and he had been shoved forward, in a most undignified manner, to the elevated throne of the bishop. To escape being smothered, he mounted the two steps of the pulpit. What a scene: sweltering, sweating Augustine stood by the bishop's throne, attempting to support himself amid deafening shrieks. He burst into tears —small wonder—for God was now laughing him to scorn; he was the one who had demeaned the priests and their congregations. "I think my Lord wanted to correct me, because, without adequate virtue and experience, I had dared to reprimand what was there being done before I had experienced the misdeeds of many clerics. . . . That was the cause of those tears."[15] Surrounding Augustine would have been benches where the priests sat, and there some pious men were placidly looking at him, reminding him of his cruel sarcasm.

Ironically the Hippo congregation jumped to the conclusion the tears were flowing so copiously because Augustine secretly longed to be a bishop, and now he would be merely a priest. But it happened. Amid nonplused yet highly dramatic circumstances, Augustine was elevated to the priesthood in 391. His ordination sermon, "To the Seekers," was especially appropriate: "Do you realize, my fellow beginners, to what delight in the Lord you will come when you cast aside the delight of the world?"[16] In another sermon, preached at this same time, he told what was in his heart:

> In consideration of my own lack of age and training, and of my inexperience in this office which I have received, and in view of my affection for you, I, who now assist as priest at this altar which you will soon approach, should not deprive you of the

ministry of a sermon. The Apostle says, "For if you confess with your mouth that Jesus is the Lord, and believe in your heart that God has raised him from the dead, you shall be saved."[17] (Romans 10:9-11)

In all likelihood, the eccentric Valerius had contrived the entire scene. Laymen may well have been posted for that particular service, knowing that Augustine would be in attendance, for Valerius had originally invited the noted orator from Tagaste to come to Hippo under pretext of discussing his latest book. It worked!

Immediately after ordination, Augustine made an urgent request of Bishop Valerius; he wished for some time for absolute quiet, for contemplation, for study of the Bible. Augustine felt ill equipped to enter so demanding a life. A priest must preach; knowledge of Scripture was essential. He wanted to be alone with books; he required "medicine"[18] for his soul:

I have since learned much, very much more than I expected. . . . I had not known the extent of my skill and strength in avoiding or overcoming them, thinking I was of some use. Then the Lord laughed at me and willed to show me myself in action.[19]

Again, Valerius demonstrated uncanny administrative ability. He granted a leave of several months for intensive Bible study. Augustine regarded it "healthy advice" and in writing to Aurelius speaks of "frequent pondering of the Sacred Books." As the years went by, Augustine became a walking Bible encyclopedia. In all, he cited Scripture 42,816 times in his writings.

Augustine returned to Hippo's demanding schedule refreshed. He had pored over the Pauline Epistles, was excited about Paul's concept of authority—an ideal rationale for ministry. Almost at once Valerius directed Augustine to preach; an innovation indeed, for only the bishop preached. Valerius knew what he was doing; he and Augustine complemented each other perfectly. Augustine always spoke of the older man with deep respect and much love, "my most blessed father." He referred to him as "a man of moderation and mildness, of prudence and vigilance in the Lord." There was no trace of envy in the old man who knew the young priest would eclipse him; he delighted in propelling Augustine as rapidly as possible.

Valerius further granted permission for the establishment of a monastery—to the gratification of Augustine. Now he had his friends: Evodius and Alypius who would become bishops. There were newcomers, such as Possidius, who in years to come would write Augustine's biography. Soon this simple fellowship became a seminary, training future priests and bishops for Africa.

As usual, Augustine was industriously writing. In 392 he completed *On the Value of Believing.* "If I were to believe, Honoratus," began the dedication, "that a heretic and a man who believes heretics were one and the same, I should think it well to rest both my tongue and my pen in the matter."[20] So he begins his work addressed to a friend "whom I knew to have been taken in by the Manichaeans and still held in that error, deriding in the discipline of the Catholic faith the fact that men were to believe but were not taught, by reason most certain, what truth was."[21]

It is another frontal attack on his bitter enemies: "For almost nine years, during which time I rejected the religion which my parents had implanted in me as a child, [I was] to follow these men and diligently to listen to them." He then proceeds to demolish the faith he once espoused: "You well know that the Manichees, by finding fault with the Catholic faith, and in chief, by tearing apart and mangling the Old Testament, stir up the unlearned."[22] We see Augustine the priest-militant, engaged in a conflict he relished. He continued his onslaught:

> And in this inquiry they do indeed often stir up their listeners to ask questions, but, when they have them fully roused, they so teach them that it would be better to sleep forever.

Here it is, their most vulnerable spot. Augustine drives the blade home.

> God is not the author of evil; He has never repented of any of His actions; He is not troubled by any stormy disturbance of the soul; His kingdom is not a little portion of the earth; He does not approve of nor does He command any sin or wickedness; and He never deceives.[23]

We now see a new facet of Augustine's personality; he is the merciless adversary who gives no quarter. He wanted to stamp out the Manichees once and for all. He decided, certainly with Valerius' approval, to meet the situation head on by challenging an old acquaintance from Carthage, Fortunatus, to a public debate. It was a judicious move; debate was Augustine's forte. In the great hall of the public bathhouse, on a sweltering August 28, A.D. 392, Augustine glared at Fortunatus: "I now think an error what I had previously thought to be the truth. Whether I am right in my opinion, I desire to hear from you."[24] For two days the polemics enthralled a huge audience of Catholics, Manichees, and all sorts of pagans and nonbelievers. On the third day Fortunatus vacated hall and city, never to return; it was a luminous victory for the Catholics. Augustine made tremendous gains in the city and in so doing served notice to all heretics and schismatics they were next. He had now established himself as the protagonist for the Catholics.

Augustine followed up his conquest with a concluding broadside: *Against Fortunatus the Manichaean*, really a record of the debate. "This discussion was recorded by stenographers." He took advantage of every opportunity:

> I have compressed this disputation into a book to serve as an historical record. In it, the question of the origin of evil is treated. I affirmed that the evil of mankind has sprung from free choice of the will; he, on the other hand, tried to show that the nature of evil is coeternal with God. But on the following day, he at last admitted that he found nothing which he could say against us.[25]

Having tasted blood, Augustine pursued his quarry in *On Free Will*, the work begun in Rome. "I completed Books II and III in Africa after I had been ordained presbyter at Hippo Regius."[26] It was on the origin of evil, and of such extent "we postponed some incidental questions, which either I could not solve or which required lengthy discussion."[27]

Augustine was engrossed in the study of Scripture. In 392 he was exceedingly anxious to have fresh renditions, so he began writing the learned Jerome in Bethlehem, asking for Latin translations of Greek commentaries. Augustine had made himself somewhat proficient in Greek, but knew scant Hebrew. While he was consummate master of Latin, other languages did not appeal. He knew enough Punic to engage in a conversation. His failure to master other tongues may have driven him to wizardry in use of native speech and understanding of translated Old and New Testaments. He felt compelled to study constantly. As late as 416, in the midst of great Councils in Carthage, he insisted upon taking five days of complete and uninterrupted retirement for study of Scripture. He wrote Jerome: "Therefore, I ask, and the whole group of students of the African Churches joins me in asking, that you would spare neither trouble nor labor in translating the books of those who have treated so well of our Scripture in Greek. You can bring it about that we, too, should have such men as those—and especially one—whom you display so freely in your letters."[28] It was the beginning of a tremendous friendship—through exchanged epistles.

Augustine was captivated by the Psalms and in A.D. 392 he had completed commentaries on the first thirty-two psalms, the beginning of his huge *Exposition on the Psalms*. This scrutiny would continue almost until the time of his death. Of Psalm 118 he later noted, "I have deferred the explanation . . . not so much because of its length, which is known to all, but because of its depth, which is recognized by few."[29]

How natural that a priest at Hippo, caring for souls during 393–396, should turn to the Sermon on the Mount. But is the Sermon realistic? Can sinful humanity put it into daily practice? "I think he will find in it," said Augustine, "as measured by the highest norms of mortality, the perfect pattern of the Christian life."[30] Out of a pastor's heart came, "I wrote two books, *On the Lord's Sermon on the Mount, according to Matthew*."[31] It is possible to live a godly life: "Further, a certain strength and ability to walk in the way of wisdom lies in good conduct persevered in until the heart's cleansing and its singleness are achieved." Exactly, and the same applies to the eye: "Once the eye has been cleansed and made single, it will be fit and capable of beholding and contemplating its own interior light."[32]

We can see the young African pastor in his study, writing very simple, practical admonitions to his flock. As an old man, reviewing the work he noted:

> It is not possible in this life for anyone to reach a state wherein "the law warring against the law of the mind" is not also present in the members, since, even if the spirit of man should resist in such a way that it does not slip into giving its consent, yet it would continue to struggle. Hence, what I said: "No

movement is rebellious against reason," can correctly be applied to peacemakers in the sense that, by subduing the concupiscence of the flesh, they eventually arrive at this absolute peace.[33]

Augustine found Genesis fascinating. "After I was now settled in Africa, I wrote two books, *On Genesis, Against the Manichaeans.*"[34] In attacking the Manichees, Augustine was defending "the Old Law" which they had rejected with such contempt. He employed Ambrose's method of allegorical meaning, and found Genesis a treasure. He later began, but never completed, *On the Literal Meaning of Genesis.* "I wanted to test my capabilities in this truly most taxing and difficult work also. But in explaining the Scriptures, my inexperience collapsed under the weight of so heavy a load and, before I had finished one book, I rested from this labor which I could not endure."[35] It is the wonderful candor that enables us to see Augustine struggling with Genesis, both loving it and finding it his nadir.

Searching the Scriptures, preaching, wrestling with errors in his bygone allegiance to Manichaeism all convinced Augustine that the Catholic Church must bestir herself. Militant infidels and misbelievers were abroad in the land. He wrote Valerius:

> If Africa should take the lead in stamping out these abuses, she ought to be worthy of imitation; but, as far as the greater part of Italy is concerned, and in all or most of the overseas churches, these practices either were never introduced, or, if they sprang up and took root, they were suppressed and destroyed by the vigilant care and censure of holy bishops, who had a true view of the life to come.[36]

It is incredible! Within so short a period a presbyter is taking upon himself the power to summon bishops to be about the work of Christ.

In December of 393 the General Council of Africa assembled in Hippo—and Africa had more bishops than any other section of the church. This august body would have comprised all the bishops of Africa. It was one of the major conclaves of the African Church and Augustine was doubtless the instigator. It was an attempt to bring the Catholics out of the doldrums. Sheer impertinence it was for a mere priest to thunder advice to bishops, but the wonder is that they listened, or perchance they perceived the flowering of genius.

On December 3, A.D. 393, Augustine addressed the Council using the theme, *On the Faith and the Creed*. It was a brilliant, stirring call for reform. Making excessive use of Scripture, he employed the symbol of the Lamp which dispels darkness and ignorance. Why should intelligent Catholics permit the Manichees to be the interpreters of the Old Testament? Let Catholics answer their critics with superior biblical knowledge and understanding. "While still a presbyter I discoursed concerning *On the Faith and the Creed* in the presence and at the bidding of the bishops who were holding a plenary Council of the whole African Church at Hippo Regius. At the earnest request of several of them . . . I wrote down my discourse in a book."[37] Point by point he examined the essence of the Catholic faith: "By the gift of God, that is, by the Holy Spirit, there was shown towards us such humility on the part of God most high that he deigned to take upon him the whole of human nature in the womb of a Virgin . . . the Word assumed the whole of human nature, body, soul and spirit. . . . The incarnation took place for our salvation."[38]

During 394 Augustine produced a spate of biblical works. In order to equip himself, for ministry at Hippo and for the coming encounter with antagonists, Augustine was ere long hard at work on Romans. He was called to Carthage to address the bishops who met in Council. "While I was still a priest, we who were in Carthage at the same time happened to read the Epistle . . . to the Romans and, after I . . . replied to certain questions asked me by some of my brethren, they wanted my reply put into writing." His *An Explanation of Certain Passages of Romans* is the result. "When I yielded to them, another book was added to my previous works."[39]

Augustine's amazing literary productivity continued with further work on Psalms. He likewise undertook Galatians: "I explained the same Apostle's Epistle to the Galatians . . . omitting some portions, but in a continuous fashion and in its entirety." *An Explanation of Galatians* deserves a reading. He remarked of one passage:

> "The flesh lusts against the spirit, the spirit against the flesh; for these are opposed to each other so that you do not what you would,"[is] applicable to those who are "under the law" not yet "under grace." For, up to this time, I had not yet realized

that these words are also applicable to those who are "under grace" not "under the law" because they, too, lust after the lusts of the flesh against which they lust in spirit; even though they do not yield to them.[40]

"Roaring Lions"—The Donatists

·During his years at Hippo, "Augustine's sermons were frequently interrupted by sheer noise coming from a neighboring church, the Donatist basilica." Who were these Donatists? The sect was born just after the horrible persecution under Diocletian (A.D. 303–305), during which there was evidence of moral slackness in the African Church. A number of Catholics renounced their faith when faced with torture. Some priests and bishops were guilty of handing over Christian Scriptures and devotional objects to the Roman authorities. These apostasies were especially prevalent in Numidia. The cowardice of some clergy was known and greatly lamented. They had failed in the moment of trial.

Once the danger of persecution subsided there was intense reaction against all *traditores*. It came to a climax when a new Bishop of Carthage was to be elected. The Archdeacon Caecilianus was hurriedly chosen, but it was gossiped that he had not only prevented faithful Christians from visiting the martyrs in their prisons, but he had joined with his bishop, Mensurius, in yielding Holy Scriptures to the pagan authorities for burning. Further, one of the three consecrating bishops was Felix of Abthugni. It was alleged that he was a *traditor*. Matters were further complicated by the fanatical opposition of the wealthy and powerful Spanish woman, Lucilla. She had been offended by Caecilianus. Bribes were offered and Caecilianus was deposed and Majorinus elected in his place. He was succeeded, in turn, by Donatus, a man of enormous energy and skill.

Caecilianus, however, did not take defeat lightly. He and his followers turned to Rome and secured a ruling from both Pope and Emperor that he had been rightfully elected. An inquiry further proved that Felix was not a *traditor*. It seemed to be a clear case for both men: they were faithful Christians.

It was now the Donatists—named for their bishop—who appealed to a Council at Rome; they were denounced. A Council at Arles even declared that the character of the one who administers the Sacraments had no bearing whatever on their validity. Baptism, Communion, and Ordination, even by a *traditor*, were valid. Donatists refused to accept the verdicts. They cited Cyprian, the great African martyr-bishop, who said that an unworthy priest could not administer the Sacraments. There was now division, open warfare between Catholic and Donatist churches—especially in Africa. Both claimed to be the *true* Christian Church. Donatists maintained they alone refused to bend the knee before Roman paganism. "It was an extra sharp attack of African individualism."[41] They were—so they claimed—the pure in morals and discipline. They made tremendous appeal to Africans, especially in Numidia. Thimgad, Bagai, and Carthage were cities where the Donatists made great gains.

Almost any method might be used by Donatists against Catholics, including a boycott at Hippo by local bakers who were not permitted to sell bread to Catholics. Donatists, claiming to be the true, uninterrupted succession of the Church of the Martyrs, must reject all renegades—Catholics. It was necessary to preserve the purity of their faith. Should a Catholic wish to become a Donatist, rebaptism was essential. These sons of the martyrs boasted of their impressive church structures, enormous basilicas, warehouses, shrines, hostels for pilgrims. Clustered around these edifices were scores of dwellings—"the flock of the Lord."

Related, sometimes very distantly, was a frightening strong arm group called the Circumcellions, "those who lived around the tent." Some conscientious Donatists disclaimed any tie. These were bands of fanatics armed with bludgeons, roaming the countryside, engaging in pillage and burning, especially of out of the way Catholic farms and homes. They did not reserve their terrifying "witness" to rural areas. Bishop Maximianus of Bagai was seized in his own basilica and stabbed while his church was being desecrated. Some of his congregation attempted to save the man only to have the Circumcellions snatch the bleeding bishop and throw him from a tower. Miraculously the man fell on a dungheap and survived.

Possidius, Bishop of Calama, had his house burned. When he fled he was captured and would have been beaten to death had not the Donatist Bishop, Crispinus—who was fearful of a charge of murder—interfered. One practice was for Circumcellions to enter a Catholic Church and "purify" it by scraping the walls, scrubbing the floors, then drenching it all with water. The altar would be destroyed and salt poured where it once stood. Individual Catholics frequently were apprehended and their eyes were plastered with lime and salt.

Augustine, too, was threatened by the Circumcellions. During one trip he accidentally took a wrong road. It saved him from ambush and death. There were constant stories of the midnight attacks, the maiming of Catholics amid shouts of "Praise to God." Nothing seemed to deter these rabid, martyrised individuals. If captured, they cried to be put to death and given martyrdom. They were a fearful group.

It did not require much time for Augustine to enter the fray against the Donatists and all who might be related to them. He wrote:

> There are two books of mine whose title is *Against the Party of Donatus*. . . . I said: "I am displeased that schismatics are violently coerced to communion by the force of any secular power." And truly, at this time, such coercion displeased me because I had not yet learned either how much evil their impunity would dare or to what extent the application of discipline could bring about their improvement.[42]

This is an extraordinary work, a rhythmical poem. Each stanza begins with letters of the alphabet—A to V—and is made up of twelve verses, with a recurring line, "You who take your joy in peace, now is the time to judge what's true."[43] This was but one of many attacks on a powerful adversary who insisted the church should be small, pure; the Chosen People, consummated saints. Throughout his ministry Augustine had to contend with this stubborn foe. He was constantly lampooning their theology and their moral life and demanding why their persecution of Catholics. Augustine made it clear that the validity of the sacrament did not depend on the virtue of the one administering it: "The spiritual value of a sacrament is like light; althouth it passes among the impure, it is not polluted."

In Augustine the Donatists found their most articulate, and relentless critic. For him the Catholic tradition was the true Church. It was the Donatists who had fallen away. "Why," he asked, "do you rebaptize Catholics under the pretext that their priests are traitors, and, as such, unworthy to administer the sacraments? It is Jesus' sacrifice and not the virtue of the priests that gives efficacy to baptism. If it were otherwise, of what use was the Redemption? Through Christ's voluntary death, all men are called to salvation.''

Writing

Writing became Augustine's avocation. His primary work was essentially responsibility for his flock at Hippo, but he also expressed himself through his pen. His letters of this period are literary masterpieces. They were not just instantaneous notes. Rather, they were detailed messages, usually pages in length. Sometimes he did have to rush to bring a letter to a conclusion because a friend was leaving on the tide: "The letter which my dearest son, our fellow deacon, Timothy, brought to you, was ready for his departure, when our sons, Quodvultdeus and Gaudentius, came to us with your letter."[44] Frequently there were jumbles, as "I wrote to you while my holy brother and fellow bishop Possidius, was still with us, before he sailed, but this letter, which you were so kind as to give him for me, reached me on March 27, almost eight months after my answer to you. I have no idea why my letter was so late in reaching you."[45] To Nebridius he had fitfully written: "You write that you have sent more letters than I have received.... I may not be able to keep up with you in answering, but I keep your letters with no less care than you use in multiplying them."[46]

These treatises were written on parchment: "I have answered by brief notations, as best I could, not only those of your questions which I have treated in this letter, but almost all the others, marking them on the parchment sheets on which you sent them."[47] Copies were made on an inferior paper. As a rule Augustine dictated: "I left off my interrupted dictation."[48] When writing to very distinguished persons, it was a practice to write in one's own hand, and on parchment. Augustine had offended Maximus and apologized for lack of proper formality: "Let him know that we are in the habit of writing long letters to our intimate friends, not only laymen but even bishops, in the same form in which we wrote to him. We do this to speed our correspondence, and besides, paper is more comfortable to hold when reading. Perhaps . . . he might think he has been slighted."[49]

Again, to Romanianus: "This letter points to a scarcity of paper, but does it not at least show there is plenty of parchment? I sent my ivory tablets to your uncle, with a message, but you will more readily pardon this bit of parchment. . . . I wish you would send back any tablets of mine."[50]

There was a long and exceedingly interesting correspondence with Bishop Paulinus of Nola as well as with Jerome. Many of these—and similar epistles—are tracts on theology. Augustine frequently had to answer a long list of questions from budding scholars. But he wrote, unflaggingly, in spite of illness, fatigue, pressure of business, or conditions in the community:

> Therefore I admit that I try to be of the number of those who write by advancing in knowledge, and advance by writing. Consequently, if I have set down anything with insufficient care or knowledge which is objected to, not only by others who are able to see it, but also by me, because I, at least, ought to see it afterward if I advance in learning, this should not be a matter of surprise of chagrin, but of excuse and congratulation, not because a mistake has been made, but because it has been censured. For, anyone who is willing for others to remain in error so as to conceal his own error is guilty of a most perverted form of self-love. How much better and more advantageous for him when he has made a mistake, if others whose warning frees him from error are themselves free from error. If he will not accept that, at least let him not have companions in his error![51]

He never ceased writing; over two hundred epistles survive. Presumably more were written. Here we see an absent-minded clergyman whose desk was so cluttered one letter was lost for months. Scatterbrained secretaries made incorrect copies which reached the outside world before the original was in the hands of dour Jerome. Augustine sealed these treasures with wax—a profile of a human face. Most appropriate, for we see his personality outlined in these letters.

Your letters are "easy to read because of their brevity,"[52] Nebridius wrote to Augustine. Augustine responded, "I do not like to write you on trite subjects."[53] To Maximus, "Are we dealing seriously, or do you want to joke?"[54] To Caelestinus, "How I wish I could speak with you at length!"[55] Or "Before I come to the point . . ."[56] to Maximinus. And to Licentius, "I have had a hard time finding an occasion to write to you."[57] To the leaders of the Sufes, "The infamous crime and unspeakable cruelty of your savagery shakes the earth and strikes the heavens."[58] How often he speaks of "the Church in Africa."[59] His letters are a mirror reflecting an authentic human being.

Bishop

In 395, the crafty old Valerius wrote secretly to Archbishop Aurelius of Carthage, Primate of all Africa, requesting that Augustine be consecrated coadjutor. It was a move as wise as it was unorthodox. Valerius wanted to keep Augustine in Hippo as the future bishop. Other cities would soon realize his brilliance, and might even kidnap him and make him their episcopal head, as was done now and then by African congregations.

Consecrating Augustine as bishop was not a foregone conclusion. An ugly scandal was being gossiped, and it posed no small problem. Augustine was accused of sending love potions to a very prominent matron. It is true he did send a bit of holy bread to Therasia the wife of Paulinus of Nola—but it was hardly a philter. It caused a rupture in the friendship with Paulinus, and for years tongues wagged.[60]

Megalius of Calama, Primate of Numidia, protested in the strongest language the idea of Augustine's elevation to the episcopate. Doubtless the gossip was a factor, for the story of Augustine and the eminent lady was widespread. Perhaps Augustine's Manichaean background posed the real problem for the archly conservative Megalius. Too, along with a great many African bishops the primate highly resented the flouting of the Council of Nicaea's rule that a bishop could not be consecrated prior to the death of the present occupant of the see. Also a considerable number of local African bishops frankly took umbrage at the sudden rise of an illustrious newcomer.

In the end, Megalius was won over, much to the delight of the Hippo congregation, and he was one of those who consecrated Augustine. Unhappily, the memory of the disgraceful rumor lingered in Augustine's mind for years. He wrote later to Profuturus:

> I am sure you have heard of the death of the elder Megalius. The day I am writing is almost the twenty-fourth since his burial. We wish to know whether you will now look to a successor for his see, if possible, for you have been putting it off. It there are scandals, there is also a remedy; if there are griefs, there is comfort. Meantime, we must be on guard lest hatred for anyone should seize our innermost heart. . . . Anger creeps in so subtly.[61]

Augustine was consecrated coadjutor bishop a short time before Christmas, 395. Valerius died the following year. Thus in 396 Augustine was Bishop of Hippo, and even Paulinus had the grace to call it "a boon to Christendom."

Valerius had made a far greater contribution than anyone then realized, or than history has since been willing to admit. He recognized the potential in the man Augustine and he was willing to risk some rules in order to give his protégé the opportunity he needed. For the next thirty-four years Augustine would give himself unstintingly to his office. It was from Hippo that he spoke to the Christian world.

Augustine's feeling at the time of his elevation was a very interesting mixture of misgiving and joy:

> So much did I dread being made a Bishop that when I found that God's servants were talking seriously about the reputation I had made I was careful not to go to places where I knew there was no Bishop. . . . But I came to this city to see a friend whom I thought I could win over to God's service and who might perhaps enter our monastery. I felt quite safe since a Bishop was in occupation of the see. But I was caught and made a priest, and once that step had been taken I was made a Bishop.[62]

How did Augustine regard the high office? "May God grant, then, that I may with the help of your prayers, be what you would have me to be—you who wish me well—may be, too, what He would have me be who called me and bade me assume this office. At the same time, whatever I may be, your hope must not be in me. I must speak disparagingly of myself, for I must now speak as your Bishop: I want to rejoice in you, not to be inflated by your praise."[63]

What type prelate was Augustine? An autocrat? Yes, but a kindly one when dealing with his family of priests and his fellowship of dedicated laypeople. He loved his associates, his fellow laborers, and throughout his lengthy episcopate he treasured the camaraderie. "A friend," he said, "is one with whom one may dare to share the counsels of one's heart."[64] He was a great bishop, but he remained essentially the person he always was: a man who worked with and related to people in their common quest for God.

IX

Championing a Cause

The Confessions
A.D. 396–400

"I do not propose to spend my time in the empty enjoyment of ecclesiastical dignity," Augustine wrote to Aurelius in Carthage, "but I propose to act as mindful of this—that I must give an account of the sheep committed to me."[1] Part of that accounting may have been a personal statement of his own struggle and victory. The result of his labors was a classic, his *Confessions*. Why undertake such a venture, baring his soul before the whole world and before history?

In one respect, Augustine was answering his critics—and they were legion. There was jealousy; Manichaean relationships; his personal moral life: a concubine; a Milanese prostitute. What, too, of pagan philosophy? Sometime during 397, Augustine began his *Confessions*. He addressed the work to his intimate circle at Hippo, the Servants of God; he also kept other such fellowships in mind—those he had held in Tagaste, Carthage, Milan, and Cassiciacum. In such a monastic setting there was absolute candor as well as depth. It was in that spirit that he wrote, not an autobiography, but an outpouring of praise to God. He held nothing back but at the same time made no attempt to shock nor to exploit his personal sex life merely for the sake of gaining an audience. He was not crude, never vulgar; he showed no exhibitionism.

Augustine had good precedent for the style and honesty of intimate autobiographical material; Africa was especially noted for an innermost sharing of the very marrow of life. There was, furthermore, a preoccupation with death; martyrdom was seen as the climax of a Christian's witness. The faith memoirs had become an accepted literary form, made ready by philosophers and now Christians making full use of this genre. Where were the authentic enemies for men and women of piety?[2] They were within: sin and doubt. If martyrdom could not be experienced, at least one could disclose salvation from past iniquities. Years later Augustine sent Count Darius a copy of the *Confessions* with the accompanying letter:

> Herein you have a portrait of me which will prevent you from praising me beyond my deserts; therein you have to believe me —not other people—about myself; in that mirror you can see me, you can see what I was and through my own fault. If you can find therein anything that pleases you, then in company with me praise Him whose praises for His work in me I would have men sing; but do not praise me. "He made us, not we ourselves"; rather had we made shipwreck of ourselves, had not He who made us, re-made us. And when you discover me in that volume, then pray for me that I fail not but may be brought to perfection. Pray, my son, pray; for I know well what I am saying, I know what I am asking for. Think it not something unfitting, something beyond your merits. You will be robbing me of a very great help if you do not do so.[3]

Written by one steeped in Neo-Platonic philosophy, the *Confessions*—readers having been taken into confidence—breathes a prayer of gratitude for continued guidance:

> Can any praise be worthy of the Lord's majesty? ... Man is one of your creatures, Lord, and his instinct is to praise you . . . . The thought of you stirs him so deeply that he cannot be content unless he praises you, because you made us for yourself and our hearts find no peace until they rest in you.[4]

As an older man of seventy-four, Augustine looked back over his work: "Thirteen books of my Confessions," he remarks, "as for me, they still move me, when I read them now, as they moved me when I first wrote them."[5]

"My love of you, O Lord, is not some vague feeling: it is positive and certain. Your word struck into my heart and from that moment I loved you."[6] Thus, Augustine wrote with an artless simplicity and a profound expression of personal gratitude. We see his *Confessions* marked by an introspection with rare depth, perhaps the first great Christian writing of this genre to achieve a worldwide readership. The first ten books tell of his conversion. "My sin was all the more incurable because I did not think myself a sinner. It was abominable wickedness to prefer to defeat your ends and lose my soul rather than submit to you and gain salvation."[7] God was drawing the sinner closer, even using the sin itself as a means of grace. "The path that leads us away from you and brings us back again is not measured by footsteps or milestones." It is the fourth century prodigal. "You loved him when he set out and you loved him still more when he came home without a penny."

Augustine closed book nine with the death of Monica and then in book ten moved to the reality of his conversion: "So, O Lord, all that I am is laid bare before you. Could anything of mine remain hidden from you, even if I refuse to confess it?" He continues then to describe the blessed release: "Physician of my soul, make me see clearly how it profits me to do this. You have forgiven my past sins and drawn a veil over them, and in this way you have given me happiness in yourself, changing my life by faith and your sacrament." It was God's action—grace—that accomplished this wondrous salvation. God's operation in behalf of the sinner. It is fundamental in Augustine's theology. The only contribution a sinner made was confession of his own wickedness. Redemption was entirely God's doing.

In Book 10, Augustine speaks of memory with a lingering fondness —he had an unusually vivid, responsive recall. "But when I say that the mind can experience four kinds of emotions—desire, joy, fear, and sorrow—I call them to mind from my memory." Pleasures of joy or the pain of sorrow, it is all the same, the "power of the memory is great, O Lord. It is awe-inspiring in its profound and incalcuable complexity."

Books 11, 12, and 13 delineate an interpretation of Genesis: "O Lord, since you are outside time in eternity, are you unaware of the things that I tell you?" He talks of matter, of means of creation: "What tool did you use for this vast work? You did not work as a human craftsman." In a delightful passage, Augustine enjoys a joke on those philosophers who ask, " 'What was God doing before he made heaven and earth?' " The conventional answer was "He was preparing Hell for people who pry into mysteries." Augustine disliked the frivolous. He insisted, "I unreservedly say that before he made heaven and earth, God made nothing. For if he did make anything, could it have been anything but a creation of his own creation?" He continued, "I only wish I knew everything that I could profit by knowing with as much certainty as I know that no creature was made before any creation took place." To those who ponder what God was doing, Augustine had the answer, "My advice to such people is to shake off their dreams and think carefully, because their wonder is based on misconception."[8]

"But you, who are the one God, the good God, have never ceased to do good," wrote the author of *Confessions*. "By the gift of your grace some of the works that we do are good, but they are not everlasting." How, how can one ever begin to comprehend infinity?

> What man can teach another to understand this truth? What angel can teach it to an angel? What angel can teach it to a man? We must ask it of you, seek it in you; we must knock at your door. Only then shall we receive what we ask and find what we seek; only then will the door be opened to us.[9]

Augustine's *Confessions* stands as a masterpiece in the world's devotional classics. Few works can equal its beauty of language, honesty of personal background, majestic heights of praise for the God whose mercy made the writing possible. Had Augustine written nothing else, he would have achieved literary immortality through his *Confessions*.

Doctrine

It would be a mistake to think the years 396–400 were spent exclusively in writing the *Confessions*. It is remarkable that in the midst of so important a work as the *Confessions* he found time for other major writings. Biblical commentaries continued to occupy much time. Then, in 397, he produced the first part of *On Christian Doctrine*. When later "I discovered that the books; *On Christian Doctrine*, were not completed, I chose to finish them as they were. . . . Accordingly I completed the third book. . . . I then added a last book. . . . The first three of these are a help to the understanding of the Scriptures."[10]

Augustine also put his hand to *On Various Questions to Simplicianus:* "The first two books which I wrote as a bishop are addressed to Simplicianus, bishop of the Church in Milan who succeeded the most blessed Ambrose. They deal with various questions. I put into the first book words where Paul shows that 'the flesh wars against the spirit' I have explained as though he were describing a man still 'under the law' and not yet living 'under grace.' Long afterwards, to be sure, I thought—and this is more probable—that these words could also refer to the spiritual man.''[11]

In 400 Augustine completed part one of his monumental *On the Trinity:* "In my youth I began a work on the Trinity, the supreme and true God; I have finished it in my old age.''[12] It was his answer to the Arian view that God is one and never in three Persons. Not only is this one of the oldest Christian theological issues, but one of the most important. What of Jesus, and the Holy Spirit? How do they relate to the Father? The question was settled by the Council of Nicaea in 325 only to be raised repeatedly. Augustine began with interpretation of Scripture, assuming absolute equality of the Godhead: all three are equal Persons.

> In this Trinity there is absolute equality. In divinity the Father is not greater than the Son; nor are the Father and the Son together greater than the Holy Spirit; nor is any single Person of the three anything less than the Trinity itself.[13]

In establishing his case, Augustine the lawyer displays consummate skill in use of illustration, logic, finesse with words. Let him speak for himself:

> Nothing draws your love but what is good. Good is earth with its lofty mountains, its gentle hills, its level plains. Good is the beauteous and fertile land, good is the well-built house with its symmetry, its spaciousness and light. Good are the bodies of living things, good is the temperate and wholesome air, good is the pleasant and healthful food, good is health itself free from pain and weariness. Good is the human face with its regular features, its cheerful expression, its lively colouring; good is the heart of a friend whose comradeship is sweet and whose love is loyal; good is a righteous man, good is wealth for the things it can enable us to do, good is the sky with its sun, moon, and stars, good are the angels of holy obedience; good is the speech that instructs the hearer winningly and counsels him appropriately, good is the poem of musical rhythm and profound thought. But enough! . . . Take away "this" and "that," and

> look if you can upon Good itself: then ·you will see God. . . .
> The soul must needs seek that Good. . . . And what is that
> Good but God?[14]

There is the delightful story of Augustine, as he labored through *On
the Trinity,* that he walked on the beach at Hippo. He saw a handsome
little boy (really an Angel in disguise) digging a hole in the sand, then
filling it with water from a cockle shell. When the bishop inquired what
the child was doing, the reply came that he was attempting to empty
the sea. "Impossible," said the bishop. "Not more impossible, Augustine," said the boy, "than for your finite mind to comprehend the mystery of the Trinity."

Augustine also wrote *On the Gospels,* "certain explanations of
some passages from the Gospel according to Matthew and others, similarly, of that according to Luke."[15]

The same year saw the completion of *On the Work of Monks.*
"Necessity forced me to write . . . the fact that, when monasteries began to be founded at Carthage, some monks who were obedient to the
Apostle were making a living by manual work, but others wanted to so
live on the alms of the faithful that, although they were doing nothing
to possess or obtain necessities, they thought and boasted that they, in a
better way, were fulfilling the precept given to the Apostles. . . . 'Look
at the birds of the air and the lilies of the field.' As a consequence . . .
there began to arise violent quarrels." The quarrels became so inflamed
Aurelius "bade me to write something on this question."[16] Lazy or stu-
pid Christians always annoyed Augustine, especially when they were
members of an Order.

Another writing *Against Faustus, the Manichaean* was a counter-
blast against Faustus "who, in blasphemous fashion, was attacking the
Law and the Prophets, and their Lord, and the Incarnation of Christ."
Augustine admits, "I wrote a lengthy work."[17]

One is exhausted merely reading a list of so many protracted,
and important works. Some, but not all, are magnificient pieces—Augustine did have a tendency to be uneven in writing. Nonetheless, a
lesser figure would have been content with literary athanasia achieved
through any one of the above. One wonders why he wrote so much.
Nobody debates Augustine's unmistakable intellectual prowess. Yet, it
is quite feasible that this enormous literary output was in pursuit of ad-

justment in personal life. He had not planned to be a priest, much less a bishop. Is his dream of disciplined study amid pleasant surroundings of the small Tagaste estate—now impossible—yet conveyed through his pen? Knotty administrative problems did not appeal to him. Was writing an outlet for his frustration? He had come to terms with the Christian gospel and at the same time not forgotten Plato his intellectual mentor. A sinful past became an illustration of the power of a God of grace who redeems. All these became important elements, grist for his mill, as he delivered his message to his time.

Augustine alchemized much of basic life. How honestly he speaks of sexual temptations, even extending them to the blessed Paul:

> For since Scripture so constantly calls idolatry fornication, and the Apostle Paul calls avarice by the name of idolatry, who can doubt that every evil concupiscence is rightly called fornication, since the soul disregards the higher law by which it is ruled and prostitutes itself as for a price through base delight in lower natures and so completes its corruption? Whoever, therefore, perceives some carnal pleasure rising in rebellion against his better desire through habit of sin, and that if it is not checked it will use violence and drag him into captivity, let him reconcile as best he can what peace he has lost by sinning and let him cry out: Unhappy man that I am, who shall deliver me from the body of this death? The grace of God, by Jesus Christ.[18]

What a bold assertion, relating those persistent human, fleshly transgressions to angelic biblical personalities. It was not done in the church. In Platonic thought there had been the ideal of overcoming flesh through contemplation through philosophy itself. Now Augustine views the problem in a new light:

> Whoever thinks that in this mortal life a man may so disperse the mists of bodily and carnal imaginings as to possess the unclouded light of changeless truth, and to cleave to it with the unswerving constancy of a spirit wholly estranged from the common ways of life—he understands neither what he seeks, nor who he is who seeks it.[19]

Augustine is now the realist. His perfectionist views have been dispelled by brutal facts of life. More and more he is drawn to Paul as he cried out to his Redeemer, "Who could I find to reconcile me to you?

Ought I to have sought the help of the angels? . . . a mediator between
God and man must have something in common with God and something in common with man."[20] Again he cries out, "Terrified by my
sins and the dead weight of my misery, I had turned my problem over
in my mind and was half determined to seek refuge in the desert. But
you forbade me to do this and gave me strength by saying: *Christ died
for us all.*"[21]

As he wrestled with the cardinal doctrinal considerations of sin
and grace, Augustine wrote to Simplicianus in Milan and received an
interesting response: " 'I have hated Esau!' " Did God say that?
Why? It became for Augustine a question of individual human
destiny. He was driven increasingly to man's utter dependence on
God. God takes the initiative, even in a would-be believer's earliest
desire for holiness, as Paul said, "For it is God which works in you
both to will and to do his good pleasure."[22] It is as though Augustine
has now come to accept his own limitations—his humanness. Whatever is accomplished, it is God working through a ransomed sinner.
In spite of what he has been, now he is totally in the employ of the
God who delivers the captive.

> The fact that those things that make for successful progress to-
> wards God should cause us delight is not acquired by our good
> intentions, earnestness and the value of our own good will—but
> is dependent on the inspiration granted us by God. . . . Surely
> our prayers are, sometimes, so lukewarm, stone-cold, indeed,
> and hardly prayers at all: they are so distant in our thoughts that
> we do not even notice this fact with pain—for if we were even
> to feel pain, we would be praying again.

While Augustine may have come to terms with his own incomplete-
ness in life, what of mankind in general? Is Augustine asking too much
from the rank and file Christian?

> This choice of God is certainly hidden from us. . . . Even if it
> should be perceptible to some men, I must admit that, in this
> matter, I am incapable of knowing. I just cannot find what crite-
> rion to apply to deciding which men should be chosen to be
> saved by grace. If I were to reflect on how to weigh up this
> choice, I myself would instinctively choose those with better in-
> telligence or less sins, or both; I should add, I suppose, a sound

and proper education. . . . And as soon as I decide on that, He will laugh me to scorn.[23]

Augustine the philosopher has shifted to the Augustine of faith, bishopric and church, but richness of the past has not been forgotten. When he became a Christian, the only commodity Augustine renounced was his sin.

> When I set before the eyes of my heart, such as they be, the intellectual beauty of Him out of whose mouth nothing false proceeds, though my weak and throbbing senses are driven back where truth in her radiance does more and more brighten upon me, yet I am so inflamed with love of that surpassing comeliness, that I despise all human considerations which would recall me thence.[24]

Augustine the Bishop A.D. 400–410

Hippo Regius was no mean city. Not only was it a major African port, it was a center for grain transport. The cosmopolitan atmosphere was just what Augustine needed as he ministered and wrote. He lived in the Christian Quarter, and there was his Basilica of Peace, the baptistry, a chapel, the bishop's house and garden, the monastery. Near at hand were villas of the very rich, "the house of the noble and illustrious youth, Julian, which adjoins our walls."[25] In all, the city boasted a population of some thirty thousand.

Augustine would have seen people from all parts of the Mediterranean world. He mentions Greek sailors and Syrians. Nearness to the sea and the availability of ships was a blessing for dispatching of letters, and he became impatient at delay caused by bottled up harbors during war times.

Africa was the breadbasket for Italy. Grain and olive oil and wine were major commodities, sent throughout the empire. There was heavy trade in the city; a great deal of coming and going. And there was wealth.

Hippo reflected Roman paganism centuries old. It had been a Roman City for some two hundred years. Naturally there were reminders everywhere of Classical culture. The theatre seated five to six thousand; there was a great public bath; the huge forum was crowded with statues, and there were hundreds of Latin inscriptions. Augustine does mention—when writing about Cicero's works—that "I should doubtless not be able to find a copy."[26] Paganism was now seen in the glorious remains: in stone, in statue, in inscription rather than in daily conversations of the people.

It was in this Hippo that Augustine lived. He was a homebody, detesting travel—save when absolutely neccessary to attend a Council—for it was a burden. Even more, he feared the sea and so when making a trip to Carthage he rode a mule. Better that torture than navigating the rocky coast of North Africa. "Because of my constitution and my state of health, I have never been able to bear the cold," he wrote to friends, "but never could I have felt storms more keenly than I did this last dreadful winter, because they made it impossible for me, I will not say to go, but to fly, to you, when you were so close to me." He goes on "I could have enjoyed being in my own natural birthplace,"[27] but even seeing Tagaste would not prompt him to travel. When he did go to Carthage, summoned by Aurelius, he followed the Mejerda Valley—a tiresome venture.[28]

Augustine's health was something of a problem, "for reasons connected with the duties of my office, such as have often obliged my holy brothers . . . to undergo hardships on the sea and across the sea. From these latter I have been excused, not through any lack of zeal, but because my health was not robust enough."[29] In a letter to Profuturus he goes to considerable length to delineate his delicate condition: "I am well; but, in body, I am in bed, for I can neither walk nor stand nor sit because of the pain and swelling of hemorrhoids and chafing."[30]

Travel, and the bothersomeness thereof, was due to Hippo's being superintended from Carthage. Many important laymen lived there and Augustine had to see them from time to time. As far as the countryside around Hippo, Augustine and the Catholic Church did not seem greatly concerned. The many wandering tribes of the hinterland were, seemingly, not part of the missionary activity of the church. These areas were looked upon as quite primitive—as indeed they were. This was a particular kind of sequestration—Hippo was self-contained. It did not feel a need for that desert world. This was an unrealistic view which would change as time and adversity spoke.

As bishop, Augustine held a major office as ancient judge in the guise of Old Testament patriarch. He had to listen to family bickerings. He spent hours attempting to be impartial. He always wore a simple black robe with a hood, a *birrus*, the garb of a layman, a Servant of God. It was for a purpose. This was a time of ostentatious dress. Romans had forgotten the simple tunic of former years. Lavish wearing apparel was now popular: bright colors—especially the stockings worn by the men, heavy brocades, and expensive jewelry were the fashion. Augustine would have none of it. Years later he wrote:

> Somebody comes with a present of a rich silk robe. It might suit a bishop, but not Augustine, not a poor man, born of poor parents. Men would only say that I had now come into expensive clothes, such as I could never have had in my father's house, or in my secular career. I tell you, an expensive robe would embarrass me: it would not suit my profession, nor my principles; and it would look strange on these old limbs, with my white hairs.[31]

He was wise. His modest dress gave simply dignity. For the same reason he also had his head shaved a great deal of the time.

The earliest surviving portrait of Augustine is a fresco in the Lateran Library, dated c. A.D. 600. We see him thoughtfully turning the pages of a huge book. His clothing is conservative, restrained: tunic, pallium, and sandals—he almost appears to be barefoot. He is not wearing the robes of a bishop. He is the scholar, a bishop of unpretentious demeanor. The Latin inscription: "Different Fathers [are noted for saying] different things but this [Father] said everything with Roman eloquence, thundering forth mystic meanings."[32]

Much of Augustine's time was spent in quasi-judicial matters. So he freely advised Marcellinus:

> As a Christian judge, you must play the part of a loving father, you must show anger for wrong-doing, but remember to make allowance for human weakness; do not indulge your inclination to seek vengeance for the vile acts of sinners, but direct your effort to the cure of the sinners' wounds.

He continued, describing Roman justice:

> Do not lose that fatherly care which you maintained throughout the inquiry, when you secured the confession of such monstrous

crimes, not by stretching the defendants on the rack, nor by tearing them with hooks, nor by burning them with fire, but by beating them with rods—a form of discipline used by school-masters, by parents themselves, and often even by bishops in their courts.[33]

A letter from Marcellinus reveals that unkind remarks were being made about Augustine: "The question has become a much-discussed one and the cleverness of those who defame the dispensation of the Lord's Incarnation is quite well known in this group." Augustine's an-swer "will pass through many hands," therefore "it should be full in appearance and carefully worked out, a brilliant solution." One "ex-cellent landlord" had praised Augustine "with sarcastic flattery, insist-ing that he had not been at all satisfied."[34] It was all part of his work, being a Judge in Israel. He was the go-between for his people and the Roman officials. Perhaps most time-consuming was keeping order among the priests. "This case had tortured me for a long time"—two had quarreled, a community was at odds. He sent them to "the place where the body of the blessed Felix of Nola is buried" where a "divine revelation should be made."[35]

Numbers of married bishops posed problems. These men and their indolent sons frequently were wealthy landowners whose lives differed slightly from the outright pagans. Augustine wanted nothing to do with them. "There are some who hold pastoral chairs that they may shep-herd the flock of Christ, others fill them that they may enjoy the tempo-ral honours and secular advantages of their office."

Augustine's close fellowship was with those of his monastery, monks who had taken the vows of poverty, celibacy, and obedience to very strict rules, the spiritually elite. Their education was not, like Augustine, in philosophy, but rather almost exclusively in Scrip-ture. These monks, in due time, became bishops themselves. Thus, almost unwittingly, Augustine established a lifestyle which was to become prototype for the cenobite Catholic. It was an austere monas-tic routine; poverty was as essential as obedience and chastity. He re-ferred to the poor as his fellow-poor; the poor were frequently his guests.

Augustine, ever the man who required companionship of friends, had established the model fellowship experienced during his teaching days at other cities. These were likeminded companions. His widowed sister had come to Hippo as Abbess of the convent. A niece also came,[36] but these women lived strictly to themselves; there was absolute prohibition against female visitors. He even refused to converse with his sister save in the presence of a third party.

The pattern for Augustine's monastery could never be called anti-intellectual. Books were read and discussed in lengthy and lively conversation, these dialogues frequently took place in the traditional "philosopher's corner" of the lovely garden. Intense study, especially by Augustine himself, was the rule. Eventually there were so many visitors a hostel was built. His nephew Patricius joined the company.

Dining was important! It was a strict diet,[37] "It is the pure heart which makes pure food." Food was simple—vegetables and occasionally meat, a little wine—served in wood, earthenware, or common alabaster dishes, but silver spoons were permitted. But the conversation: it was anything but stark. It was of lofty themes:

> I have called the pleasure attached to eating "bearable" because it is not so intense as to be able to break off or distract our thoughts from the things of wisdom if our minds are occupied with them. For during meals not only do we frequently occupy our minds with lofty matters but we hold discussions on them, and between mouthfuls and while drinking we talk together and listen without distraction to what one another says, and if there is something we want to know or remember we can readily do so, more especially if we are read to.[38]

Gossip was contraband. To insure the ideal, Augustine had verses written on the tables:

> He who takes pleasure in slandering the life of the absent,
> Should know he is unworthy to sit at this table.[39]

Once at a meal the company forgot, and in the midst of rumormongering Augustine sternly reminded them that either the verses would have to be erased or he would be obliged to leave the table.

"I confess that I readily throw myself entirely upon their charity," wrote Augustine of his soul brothers, "especially when I am wearied with the scandals of the world."[40] Why? Is there some flaw in his personal makeup, some hidden childhood need for a mother? Many have attempted to psychoanalyze—in painfully amateurish style—an honest soul who freely expressed his need. He had been cast into a bishop's lonely role, and now, perhaps more than ever, his normal desire for support and love and understanding was increased. There were countless decisions; a thousand ideas were crying to be put on paper; sermons must be preached. In the midst of the welter of conflicts, he longed for someone to talk to—not idle chatter nor superficial colloquy:

> O Lord my God, if many offer you thanks for me and many pray to you for me. Let all who are truly my brothers love in me what they know from your teaching to be worthy of their love, and let them sorrow to find in me what they know from your teaching to be occasion for remorse. This is what I wish my true brothers to feel in their hearts . . . my true brothers are those who rejoice for me in their hearts when they find good in me, and grieve for me when they find sin.[41]

Augustine could not be accused of mealy-mouthedness regarding discipline in the Order—or the church fellowship for that matter; God judges, too:

> Nevertheless, lest dangerous contagions should spread any farther, it is a matter of pastoral necessity to separate the ailing sheep from the healthy; perhaps He, to whom nothing is impossible, will heal the ailing by virtue of the very separation. Not knowing who does, and who does not, belong to the number of the predestined, we ought to be so stirred by the spirit of charity as to will that all men be saved. We do this, in effect, when, as we come across various people, and the opportunity presents itself, we strive to bring them to this, that, justified by faith, they should have peace with God.[42]

Sin cannot be tolerated, and this applies to the Christian community and personal relationships within it. One cannot endanger one's own soul, no not even for a beloved brother: "As long as that sufficiency and that personal safety—either our own or that of our friends—is merely temporal good, it will have to be sacrificed to secure eternal life. . . . Inasmuch as we love ourselves in God, if we really love Him, we truly love our neighbors as ourselves, if, as far as we are able, we lead them to a similar love of God."[43]

Intimates within the Blessed Community are to be cherished, certainly. But—does Augustine reveal personal apprehension lest these same individuals demonstrate they are capricious? He was concerned, "For fear that your life would be left barren of any friendship, and that love bestowed upon you would fail."[44] How dreadful when a trusted companion betrays that trust. Throughout his life, Augustine was chary —those close to him might prove false. He seemed to fear a possible Judas might lurk in the shadows. Never one to hold back criticism, he bravely advocated veracity:

> Dissension, however, is never to be loved. Sometimes, it is true, it arises from love or is a test of love. It is not easy to find anyone who likes to be reproved. And where is that wise man of whom it is said: "Rebuke a wise man and he will love [you]"? Surely, then, we ought not to refrain from reproving and correcting our brother that he may not heedlessly risk death ... a man is cast down for a short time while he is being re-proved, that he resists and fights back, but afterwards he reflects in solitude where there is no one but God and himself, ... he does not repeat the act which was justly censured, but now loves the brother, whom he sees as the enemy of his sin.[45]

One cannot avoid asking, did this dictum apply to Augustine himself? How did he regard criticism from the fellowship? In writing Jerome, Augustine frequently seemed to go out of his way to stir up strong feelings. In one exchange Jerome wrote acidly to Augustine, "Do not imagine that you are the only one who can quote from the poets; remember ... the popular proverb about the tired ox setting his foot down more heavily. I have dictated this with sorrow. How I wish I might deserve to embrace you, and that we might teach or learn something by mutual conversation!"[46] To Jerome's amazing candor, Augustine replied with charm,

> Therefore, if you seem to be an ox, wearied with age of body, perhaps, but still, with active mind, laboring with fruitful toil on the Lord's threshing-floor, here I am; it I have said anything wrong, set your foot down strongly. The weight of your age should not be burdensome to me so long as the chaff of my mistake is threshed out.[47]

But this communication is to the celebrated Jerome, translator of Scripture. It is not addressed to some little known African monk. In all his insistence on straightforwardness in camaraderie, one detects a certain paternalism. He never forgot he was a bishop. On the other hand, when writing his old friend Aurelius (whom he had known in Carthage in 388 as a deacon) and was elevated to Primate presiding at the various African Councils, Augustine makes a point of absolutely correct, formal address: "I have received no letter from your Reverence since we parted from each other in the flesh, but now I have read the letters of your Benignity."[48] Of course, it was a style of the times, but Augustine was adroit.

Even so, Augustine's priests were his personal treasures:

> Whence is the ardor of brotherly love kindled in me, when I hear that some man has borne bitter torments for the excellence and steadfastness of faith? And if that man is shown to me with the finger, I am eager to join myself to him, to become acquainted with him, to bind myself to him in friendship. . . . I love therefore the faithful and courageous man with a pure and genuine love.[49]

As expected, from the original coterie at Hippo, the new bishops dispersed—Severus, Possidius, Evodius, Alypius (who became Bishop of Tagaste), Profuturus. The thought of meeting these comrades at a Council made even travel bearable.

Friendship of another dimension was found with noted personalities, men of affairs with whom he could clash. "Come, then, at my request, and undertake a written debate with me," Augustine entreated Jerome, "for I should not like the silence and inactivity of our pens to complete the separation caused by physical absence."[50]

Another letter to Jerome speaks bitingly of personal relationship: "I have heard that my letter has reached you, but, as I have not deserved an answer, I do not blame this on your lack of love—no doubt there has been something to prevent it." Augustine could be curiously tactless, and yet careful to stay within the bounds of propriety. He continues in a rather sententious vein:

> I realize that I must beg the Lord to give you the inclination and opportunity of sending what you write. . . . If some chance statements are found in some of my writings, in which I am found to have different views from yours, that is nothing against you. . . . Not only am I most ready to receive in a brotherly

spirit any contrary opinion you may have to anything in my
writings to which you take exception, but I ask and insist that
you do so, and I will take pleasure in my own correction and
your goodness.

In an outburst, we can hear him cry for a face-to-face discussion:

Oh, if only it were possible for me—if I cannot live with you as
a neighbor—at least to enjoy you in the Lord, in sweet and frequent converse! But, since this is not granted to us, I ask this,
that you also may wish our being together in Christ to be, as far
as possible, preserved and increased and perfected, and that you
do not scorn to answer us, however seldom.[51]

In another letter, Augustine cannot understand why the scholar of
Bethlehem is indignant at another churchman. Why can't they compose
differences?

I confess that I felt a deep grief when I learned that such a
great evil of discord has arisen between two such dear and intimate persons, united by a bond of friendship, so well known
to all the churches. . . . What friend is not to be feared as a
future enemy, if that which we mourn could come about between Jerome and Rufinus? . . . If I could—moved with fear
and grief as I am—I would kneel at your feet, I would weep,
and with all the strength and all the love I have I would beg
each one of you . . . not to publish in writing statements
which would make it impossible for you to be friends
again. . . . It is a matter of deep and sad perplexity that such
enmity can come out of a friendship of that sort. But it will be
a much greater joy to bring about a return from such estrange-
ment to former intimacy.[52]

Sometimes Augustine enjoyed those who chided him: "As for
me," he wrote to Severus, Bishop of Milevis, "when I am praised by
one who is very kind and dear to my soul, it is as if I were praising
myself. And you must see how irksome that must be even when what
is said is only the truth. It is precisely because you are my other self
and that we form together but one soul, that you deceive yourself in
thinking that you see in me things which are not there, as a man de-
ceives himself about himself."[53]

In an altogether different context, and writing to one who, in later
years proved to be Augustine's nemesis, he says:

When by God's gift we live by the true faith, God himself is present, to enlighten the mind, to overcome concupiscence, to bear affliction. For all this is rightly done when it is done for His sake, that is, when He is loved for no reward; but love such as this cannot be ours, except it be from Him. For the rest, when a man is much pleased with himself, and puts his trust in his own powers, if he surrenders to the desires of his pride, this evil will be increased the more in proportion as the other lusts have abated in him, and pandering to that one, he restrains them as if he were laudable in so doing.[54]

Augustine may be one of the few personalities who understood rudeness, both in himself and in others. Maybe he saw through it and was brave enough to say so.

Preaching

It was within his Basilica of Peace—which literally means African Basilica—as preacher that Augustine was preeminently the African Bishop. "What joy have we in such crowds? Hear me, you few. I know that many listen to me, few take notice."[55] His congregation stood, men on one side, women on the other. Some of the women were overdressed, with painted faces, eyebrows blackened, jewels in their ears. A marble balustrade separated the widows and consecrated virgins whose faces were covered by black or purple veils. African congregations were exceedingly responsive, applauding, interrupting, voicing approval or dissent, especially when Scripture was quoted. Once Augustine was reading a translation by Jerome in which *ivy* was substituted for *vine*, and the people roared their disapproval. They frequently joined in quoting the passages and cried, "Thanks be to God" and "Praised be Christ."

During a service Augustine remained seated on his throne—*cathedra*—some fifteen feet from the nearest worshipers, at eye level. It was intimate communication. Once when he realized he had passed the hour for dining, and could hear stomachs rumble, he smiled, "Go, my very dear brothers and sisters, go and restore your strength. . . . Go then and restore your bodies so that they may do their work well, and

when they are restored, come back here and take your spiritual food."
Again, he knew his sermon was too lengthy for a sweltering congregation: "I can tell by the smell I must have preached a long while
today."

Augustine preached extempore, the message taken down by
scribes during the service, or dictated subsequently by Augustine
himself. "I see in what crowds you have come; and you see how I
am perspiring." He noted of one sermon, "I preached it to the people, and after I had preached it I wrote it."[56] On the Feast of Saints
Peter and Paul, "I feel somewhat sad," he commented, "for I do not
see so big a congregation as there should be on the feast of the Passion of the Apostles."

On rare occasions Augustine was inordinately brief. His sermon on
Stephen was only eleven lines, but the setting was dramatic. He placed
before the congregation a well known cripple who had been recently
cured by the saint. He also had carefully studied, and may have had
available, a booklet recording Stephen's miracles:

> We are accustomed to hear read the story of the miracles God
> wrought at the prayers of the Blessed Martyr, Stephen. Today
> the 'book' is the sight of this man; instead of a writing here is
> evidence; instead of paper you have his features. You who re-
> member what you used to see with grief in him, read now in
> him as he stands before you what will fill you with joy as you
> look. Give, then, more abundant glory to God, and let what is
> written in this 'book' be graven too in your memories. You
> must pardon me if I do not preach you a longer sermon; you are
> aware of my fatigue. It is due to the prayers of St. Stephen that
> I was able to do yesterday all I did while fasting and yet not
> break down, and that I should be able to speak to you at all to-
> day.[57]

The question remains: was the brevity of this sermon accidental, or was
it skillfully and powerfully designed? The latter is doubtless the case.
Augustine was a master thespian who could employ drama with maxi-
mum effect.

Augustine once spied a Manichaean present, changed his sermon
entirely, and the heretic was gloriously converted.[58] Sometimes the

bishop complained that he found the flock dull, and he frequently went to considerable length to explain the meaning of words. "The book *On the Christian Combat*, which contains the rule of faith and precepts for living, was written in simple language for the brethren who were poorly versed in the Latin tongue."[59]

While preaching in Carthage, on the theme of peace, he directed the people, "Now all say after me, 'Charity from a pure heart' [1 Timothy 1:5]" and the congregation chorused it after him. He was a master of audiences and quoted Cicero, "To teach people is needful, to delight then is a pleasure, to win them is victory."[60]

"A short Psalm but a long sermon," he remarked after preaching on Psalm 120. Aware of his loquacity, he commented, "I may have wearied some of you with all this toil. . . . There is to be another sermon tomorrow, so come with hungry maws and devout hearts." He frequently preached each morning and sometimes several times during the day. One day there were few at church, but a huge crowd at the circus: "So much the better! This will give my voice a rest." The timbre of his voice was not unusually loud or strong but surely it must have been pleasing, even musical. "My brothers, you like to come to hear me, but what is it you like? If it is I, even that is good because I wish you to love me, but I do not wish to be loved for myself."[61]

But he loved them, his faithful people. "The African Christians are best,"[62] he said! He was at home—he knew it—and he made his congregation feel likewise. "Alleluia is praise of God. To us as we labour it signifies the activity of our rest. For when after those labours we come to that rest, the praise of God will be our sole occupation, our activity there is Alleluia."[63]

Augustine mastered the art of communicating to people—both to his congregations and to acquaintances—ancient biblical truths in almost childlike unadornment. He interpreted the turning of the water into wine with a rustic reference to irrigation of the vineyard: the water eventually becomes wine.[64] He mirrored life, not as some stilted dilettante, but in poignant, earthy expressions. Sturdy sinners flocked to hear him because he gave them hope for redemption. Angelic souls stood in the congregation and wept for he reminded them that they were also transgressors in need of absolution.

Brethren, remember from what the wine is made. Many grapes hang on the vine, but the juice of the grapes is mingled into a unity. Thus also has Christ the Lord designated us. He willed that we should belong to Him, and consecrated the mystery of our peace and of our unity on His table.[65]

Demolishing the Donatists

From the beginning of his priesthood, Augustine's perception of the office of bishop was essentially that of protector and interpreter of doctrine. "You must know," he had written Valerius, "through the authority of the character you bear [you] . . . can heal by the authority of councils and by your influence the many carnal taints and weaknesses which the Church in Africa suffers in many and bewails in few."[66]

Thus, as bishop, one of his first actions was to protest celebrations on the anniversaries of the martyrs. Perhaps he remembered Ambrose's prohibition regarding meals served picnic style at tombs of the dead. In 394 Augustine abolished the *laetitia* of Saint Leontius of Hippo—first martyred bishop of the city. It was an unpopular move and required courage. "I did not rouse their tears by mine, but I admit that, after saying such things, I was overcome by their weeping and could not restrain my own. So when we had wept together, I finished my sermon with the fullest hope of their amendment." He had read to them from Ezekiel 33:9, "The watchman is held guiltless if he warn of danger, even if those who are warned will not heed."[67] He was also prepared to rend his clothes in the presence of all.

Why this stress on martyrs? Augustine's motivation may have been his relentless opposition to the Donatists. He became the warrior-bishop out to do battle in Christ's name in behalf of the Church. Sound doctrine was essential, and Donatism was a pestiferous root to be dislodged from the Lord's Vineyard. They did not even read the same translations of the Bible! Augustine loved the Songs of Africa, and these were too precious to be wasted on unbelieving ears. Africa must be rid of this apostasy.

Augustine was continually excoriating the Donatists, reminding them of the havoc wrought by the Circumcellions: "Why do you not tear off those wretched animal skins, the sign of cowardly slavery, and

put on Christian confidence,'' he wrote to Maximinus, a Donatist
bishop. He pleads for the healing of "members which lie wretchedly
wasted with disease throughout all Africa." He continues, "Let there
be an end to the terror of the bands of Circumcellions. Let us really
take action, according to reason and the authority of the Divine Scriptures, . . . may it thus be possible . . . [to] begin the destruction in our
lands of the disgrace and impiety of many parts of Africa."[68] Put an
end to this vendetta.

There was a completely false note in everything the Donatists said
and did. It was the ruination of the African people. In a letter to Euse-
bius, another Donatist bishop, Augustine pours out his wrath:

> What, I ask you, could be more detestable than what has now
> happened? An insane youth is corrected by his bishop for hav-
> ing frequently beaten his mother, and for having laid impious
> hands on her. . . . He treatens this same mother with his inten-
> tion of going over to the Donatist sect, and says that he will
> kill her, whom he is accustomed to beat with such unbeliev-
> able fury. He threatens her; he goes over to the Donatist sect;
> in his wrath, he is rebaptized, raging against his mother's life,
> he is clothed in a white garment; he is admitted within the
> sanctuary as a prominent and noteworthy person; to the grief
> of all, although he is known as a man who intends to murder
> his mother, he is displayed as if he were newly cleansed by
> baptism.
> Can you approve of this, eminent sir?[69]

Events had not moved in Catholic favor. Count Macarius, the imperial commissioner for Africa, had not helped the Catholic cause
when in 347, on royal order, he had taken the Catholic side and persecuted the Donatists. This only served to give them greater sense of
martyrdom, an image of the persecuted. Julian the Apostate had
brought a sudden change, 361–363. He was last of the pagan emperors,
and under him—strange to say—Donatists came into favor and
Catholics suffered. But this was all in the past. Now Augustine became
the spokesman for Catholics. In response to the accusation that
Donatists suffered under Macarius, Augustine pointed to the outrages
perpetrated by the Circumcellions on Catholics. He also pointed to
Gildo, Count of Africa, who was a pagan and had to be suppressed by

the Emperor Honorius. One of the outstanding Donatist bishops, Optatus of Timgad, had been friendly with Gildo—probably no more than a political alliance—but Augustine used it with telling effect. Optatus was the ally of a *pagan*!

It was at Councils in Carthage, first in 401 later in 403, that Augustine had his supreme moment. With absolute aplomb he asked, "For what am I? Am I the Catholic Church?. . . It is enough for me to be within it. You [Donatists] slander my past evil ways. You think this a great thing to do, do you? I am more severe on my own misdeeds than ever you have been. You raked them up: I have condemned them. These belong to the past. . . . Brothers, say to the Donatists just this: 'Here is Augustine . . . a bishop of the Catholic Church. . . . What I have learned to look to above all, is the Catholic Church. I shall not put my trust in any man.' "[70] Another Council followed in 404 and requested Roman police protection against marauding Circumcellions. To illustrate the sheer brutality, Augustine played to the gallery—unfairly perhaps—by use of idle tales. He composed a popular song which embraced, among other legends, the story of the aged Catholic bishop who was forced to mount his own altar and dance with dead dogs tied around his neck.[71]

As the contest with the Donatists increased in gravity, Augustine began to stress discipline as part of the makeup of the true church, making it necessary to use coercion to bring about order and commitment. The alternative was chaos:

> The reigns placed on human licence would be loosened and thrown off: all sins would go unpunished. Take away the barriers created by the laws! Men's brazen capacity to do harm, their urge to self-indulgence would range to the full. No king in his Kingdom, no general with his troops, . . . no husband with his wife, no father with his son, would attempt to put a stop, by any threats or punishments, to the freedom and the sheer sweet taste of sinning.[72]

In June 405 the "Edict of Unity" was promulgated; Donatists were branded as heretics. It was a victory, of sorts, for Catholics. As Augustine rejoiced, the Donatists claimed he was rejecting his loudly trumpeted position on freedom of the will. In large part they were correct. It is easy to see how he moved; he was now stressing the fallen state of man with only God's grace to save. As imposed discipline was good for man the sinner, Roman authority was bringing necessary order our of the wild disarray of Donatism. "There are some who think that the Christian religion ought to be ridiculed rather than upheld," insisted Augustine. He went on:

> The reason for this is that in it, not the thing which may be seen is set forth, but faith in things which are not seen is imposed upon men. For the sake of refuting those who, prudent in their own opinion, seem to be opposed to believing what they cannot see, we surely have not the power to present to the eyes of men the divine truths which we believe.[73]

The wrangle continued. It was on August 25, 410 that the Emperor Honorius, cautious lest he lose Catholic support, summonsed Catholic and Donatist bishops for a summit conference. At last Augustine's moment had come. He could meet them in an official forum. The renown Marcellinus, a faithful Catholic layman, as Imperial Commissioner, would preside, hear both sides, then render a decision. The disputations would be in Carthage. There were three sessions, June 1–8, 411, meeting in the public bath. Only seven bishops from each side were to speak, but a great mass of Donatist prelates—some 284—intruded. It was a year later that Augustine and other Catholic bishops of the Council of Zerta wrote in imperious fashion to the Donatists:

> We came to Carthage, your bishops and we, and we met together—something which yours had been refusing to do, saying that it was beneath their dignity. Seven representatives were chosen on each side, yours and ours, to speak in the name of all. Seven others on each side were chosen to act as advisers, when the need should arise. Then, four on each side were named to watch over the writing of the records, so that no one could say they had been tampered with in any way. Besides that, four stenographers were allotted from each side, by us and by them, to take turns, two and two, with the judge's secretaries, so that no one of us could allege he had said something which had not been taken down.[74]

Augustine was silent during all sessions, until the last and concluding moment, when he personally moved forward to administer the *coup de grace*. As the expert in debate, he demolished his opposition. Early the morning of June 9, 411, Marcellinus delivered his verdict: Donatists were misbelievers, their basilicas were closed, and those who were faithful had to go underground. They were cast out. Not only was it complete triumph for Catholic forces; it was also a personal victory for Augustine. Even more, righteousness prevailed. He later observed, "As light and darkness, piety and impiety, justice and iniquity, sin and right-doing, health and feebleness, life and death, are contraries, so too are truth and falsehood."[75]

The Pelagian Controversy A.D. 410–420

Augustine insists that he wanted to spend his latter years free from controversy. There had been excessive disharmony, and he hoped for a relatively tranquil diocese. Such would never be the case, however, for it was not Augustine's makeup. Now a new antagonist appeared: Pelagius. Perhaps it was the most difficult of all controversies, yet it produced major writings and, above all, established a major doctrinal thesis—the nature of man: is he good or evil? It provided Augustine with a gratifying impetus for hard work.

Pelagius was a monk of Celtic background, a brilliant man of highest moral character. He had studied extensively; his writings reflect tremendous insight and learning. He visited Rome in 400 and was shocked by the ethical collapse of a so-called Christian culture. He immediately preached a powerful appeal for righteous responsibility— Christians ought to live as though answerable to God. He could not have come to Rome at a more opportune time. The city was crying for a fresh voice, and he became that latter-day prophet. Numbers of outstanding Romans responded enthusiastically and, shortly, Pelagius became popular.

Pelagius intrepidly denied original sin. Man, he said, could sin, and sin repeatedly; but it was a matter of individual choice. Each human being was responsible for his own sins. Adam was a sinner, but that was the extent of it—an individual who committed a violation of God's ordinances. Mankind did not fall with him. Human nature remained intact, just as it had come from the Creator's hand. Mankind, therefore, was basically good; there was no fallen race; only individual sinners.

Thus, for Pelagius, humanity did not need redemption, only inspiration. Jesus, consequently, came as master and model, not Savior. Christ becomes the paradigm: the moral example for all men. Pelagius conceptualized a similar role and function regarding the church. In baptism the Christian receives a higher generation, not regeneration. Sacraments thus become tokens, symbols of what man can and ought to do within himself.

In denial of original sin and man's hereditary guilt, Pelagius further concluded that physical death is, in reality, but a part of nature—not the penalty for nor the result of sin. Spiritual death is not the inherited consequence of Adam's sin, but it comes to each individual who misuses the power of free choice. All humans, by virtue of their free will, have the ability to avoid making unrighteous selections. In the exercise of his free will and moral responsibility, man may grasp the aid of divine grace, which is bestowed according to man's merit.

Pelagius came to Africa, indeed to Hippo, in the hope that he might see Augustine. It was 410 and Augustine was conveniently absent from the city. Pelagius had written, and the bishop made a courteous but exceedingly cautious reply, supposedly an invitation to visit.[76] The visitation never took place. Within a year Pelagius had moved on to Palestine and Augustine knew of the learned monk only through his writings.

It was an ardent satellite of Pelagius, Caelestius, who kept the church in ferment. He had sought the priesthood but was resoundingly denied the office. Thus rejected, Caelestius redoubled his efforts and spent his years championing Pelagian views.

One of the occasions which prompted interminable discussion was a message sent by Pelagius to Demetrias in 413. She was a lady of note who elected to become a num. Pelagius wrote her "since perfection is possible for man, it is obligatory."[77] In Pelagius' eyes, it was a matter of unquestioned obedience to God; Deity demanded nothing less. "Whenever I have to speak of laying down rules for behavior and the conduct of a holy life, I always point out, first of all, the power and functioning of human nature, and show what it is capable of doing . . .

lest I should seem to be wasting my time, by calling on people to embark on a course which they consider impossible to achieve."[78] Strong, virile character is thus essential. Success will be *won*. He even went on in his bold assertion of obedience: God would condemn to the eternal fires of hell anyone who failed to perform any command, yea, any single one.

Augustine listened, then retaliated, driving his point home. How could a *sinner* perform all that the law requires? Augustine answered Pelagius on the terrors of the Last Judgment so frequently mentioned: "For, he who fears hell does not fear to sin, he fears to burn; but the one who hates sin itself as he hates hell, he is the one who fears to sin."[79]

Pelagius is clearly the ascetic. While complete freedom belongs to the individual, with it is frightening responsibility; one must answer for every sin, each action unworthy of a disciple. To do less would be to commit deliberate acts of contempt for God. It is iron will within the Christian. Augustine responded in a thoughtful and kindly way—and he was not always kind—"Many sins are committed through pride, but not all happen proudly . . . they happen so often by ignorance, by human weakness; many are committed by men weeping and groaning in their distress."[80] It is almost as though the bishop were searching his own heart. For him the church was called by God to minister to a bleeding and broken humanity, hurt and aching. Grace was the healing balm, provided by a loving, gracious God for sinners. "Man was lost by free-will," said Augustine."The God-Man came by liberating grace."[81]

Another fascinating difference between Augustine and Pelagius is reference to babies. Augustine made so many allusions to infants, to his love for them, his use of them as symbols: children of God, childlike innocence: "Can this be the innocence of childhood? Far from it, O Lord! But I beg of you to forgive it. . . . It was, then, simply because they are small that you used children to symbolize humility when, as our King, you commanded it by saying that *the kingdom of heaven belongs to such as these* ."[82] Again, "Without you I am my own guide to the brink of perdition. And even when all is well with me, what am I but a creature suckled on your milk and feeding on yourself, the food that never perishes? And what is any man, if he is only man? Let the strong and mighty laugh at men like me: let us, the weak and the poor, confess our sins to you."[83]

Pelagius scoffed at infantile terms; to consider a Christian thus was degrading, "There is no more pressing admonition than this, that we should be called *sons* of God."[84] He employed terms from Roman law. A son was absolutely liberated from his father. For Pelagius, a Christian was one who had come of age, an adult, ready to go out into the world as a gladiator, willing to do battle and die, if need be.

In responding, Augustine articulated his position on the nature of man, he likewise consummated his interpretation of God's grace. In Pelagianism he saw a dread cancerous condition within the church. Many of his fellow bishops were of another mind. They looked upon Pelagius as a sincere man—he was that indeed—and a Christian who wanted to remain a good Catholic, a reforming Catholic to be sure, but one who loved the church. It is the stereotype factionalism. Pelagius is the reformer who tries mightily to carry his point but he faces Augustine, an adversary too powerful of intellect and personality. Augustine is champion of orthodoxy, stressing man's sinful nature and God's redeeming grace. Salvation for humanity was wholly an act of God; man can merit nothing, absolutely nothing. "We prove by . . . testimonies of Sacred Scripture that God's grace is not given according to our merits."[85]

Why did Augustine not go along with a number of other ecclesiastical leaders and regard Pelagius as ultraliberal, yet keep him within the fellowship? Perhaps it results from knowing man too intimately, or better, from knowing himself too well, that Augustine kept hammering away at sin. Pelagius provides a beautiful picture of man, but is it realistic? Augustine thunders: No! Man is filled with pride, first of the three fundamental lusts, along with voluptuousness and curiosity. From pride flow greed and all other manifestations of man's inability to save himself and his world. In the end man can rely only upon God. "God has humbled himself—and still man is proud."[86]

In attempting to be fair to Augustine we must see him as one defending a faith laden with deep, personal meaning. He had experienced so great an outpouring of grace, and he was such a miserable sinner, that he could not permit someone—even one of great sincerity—to take away that essential truth as to the reality of God, man, and man's salvation.

> To praise the benefits of medicine does not imply a profit in the diseases and wounds which medicine heals. The higher our praise of medicine, the stronger is our censure and abhorrence of the hurts and diseases from which the admired art relieves us. So the praise and preaching of grace is the censure and condemnation of offences. Man needed to be shown the foulness of his malady.[87]

In Diospolis (modern Lydda) a synod of fourteen bishops met on December 20, 415, and heard Pelagius, and came to the conclusion he was essentially sound in the faith. For Augustine this was an example of the East, their almost resigned quality, their credulousness. Augustine did not remain idle. He sent Orosius to be with Jerome and to learn more about Pelagius. In September of 416, Orosius returned to Carthage where a Council was in session. Africans knew how to deal with heretics. They heard the report and took action.

A second Council was assembled in Milevis under the domination of Augustine and Alypius. Three hundred bishops unanimously agreed that Pelagius was in error. Of course, this was Augustine's doing. In no time a full report of the two African councils was dispatched to Pope Innocent, together with a personal epistle from Augustine, Alypius, and Aurelius. It was all handled with great care: "We have sent your Holiness letters from the two councils of the province of Carthage and of Numidia, signed by a large number of bishops. These letters condemn the enemies of the grace of Christ. . . . They say that human nature is free, so that they look for no liberator; and safe, so that they consider a savior superfluous; they claim that this nature is so strong of its own strength, acquired once and for all at the moment of creation, without any helping grace from Him who created it, that it can subdue and extinguish all passions and overcome all temptations."[88]

In essence, Pelagius and his disciple Caelestius—especially the latter—had six charges made against them, and these are very carefully listed: 1. Adam was made mortal and would have died whether he had sinned or not. 2. The sin of Adam injured himself alone and not the human race. 3. Newborn children are in that state in which Adam was before the fall. 4. Neither by the sin and death of Adam does the whole race die, nor by the resurrection of Christ does the whole race rise.

5. The Law leads to the kingdom of heaven as well as the gospel.
6. Even before the coming of the Lord there were men without sin.
These blasphemous errors, along with their fountainhead, Pelagius
must be denounced. Augustine was determined. Lamentably, Pope Innocent was an old man with scant thought of a doctrinal war, and he
wrote a lame reply to Africa and then on March 12, 417, summoned all
his strength and died. Zosimus, the new pope, to the consternation of
Augustine was attracted to Pelagius and Caelestius. "If only you had
been present, my beloved brethren," wrote Zosimus, "how deeply
each one of us was moved! Hardly anyone present could refrain from
tears at the thought that persons of such genuine faith could have been
slandered."[89]

Augustine bided his time, marshalled his orthodox African bishops,
wrote letters to Paulinus of Nola, to Dardanus the former Prefect of
Gaul. His most cunning move was to circulate *On Correcting the
Donatists*, in which he insisted that the full force of Roman law be directed against the Donatists. There had been riots in Rome and Pelagians had aided in attacking an elderly Roman official. Augustine's
pamphlet appeared at the strategic moment. An angry Emperor Honori-
ous issued a punitive decree on April 30, 418, denouncing Pelagius and
Caelestius as disturbers of the faith. He later expelled the two from
Rome: "It has been decreed some time ago that Pelagius and Caelestius, inventors of an unspeakable doctrine, should be expelled from the
city of Rome as sources of contamination to Christian unity, lest by
their vile persuasions they should seduce untutored minds."[90]

Zosimus expired, most conveniently, in December, 418. Under the
leadership of youthful Julian of Eclanum, an attempt was made to give
Pelagius a new trial, but Augustine and Alypius, together with Count
Valerius, blocked it. Augustine had triumphed again. "Wind bags" he
called the Pelagians and Caelestians. "Nobody in this flesh, nobody
in this corruptible body, nobody on the face of this earth, in this mal-
evolent existence, in this life full of temptation—nobody can live
without sin"[91] Perhaps the greatest writing to come out of this drawn
out controversy was *The Spirit and the Letter*: "We conclude that a
man is not justified by the precepts of a holy life but by faith in Jesus
Christ. That is to say, not by the law of works, but by that of faith; not

by the letter, but by the spirit; not by the merits of deeds, but by free grace."[92]

Augustine worked through his concept of grace—defined as the blessing of God's influence. Man stands in need of grace in order to begin, continue, and finish all the good he might ever attempt. Grace is the *only* means whereby man might overcome. Man's desire for grace indicates the presence of grace already, though man may not be aware of it. "The law was therefore given that grace might be sought; grace was given that the law might be fulfilled. Now it was not through any fault of its own that the law was not fulfilled, but by the fault of the carnal mind; and this fault was to be demonstrated by the law, and healed by grace."[93]

Is it not somewhat remarkable that a theologian who spoke so eloquently of grace could be so severe on a worthy opponent? No. Augustine was honest. In Pelagius' liberalism he saw a perilous obsession with the idea of man's natural goodness. Augustine had experienced tears, pain, blood: "Inchoate charity, therefore, is inchoate justice; progressing charity is progressing justice; great charity is great justice; perfect charity is perfect justice."[94] Thus, with clear conscience, Augustine could write these beautiful words:

> Love, and do what you will; whether you hold your peace, of love hold your peace; whether you cry out, of love, cry out; whether you correct, of love correct; whether you spare, through love do you spare; let the root of love be within, of this root can nothing spring but what is good.[95]

Yes, Augustine could write it, but is he not dangerously approaching the same unrealistic view of man for which he so harshly denounced Pelagius? Augustine would, of course, vouchsafe that such love comes only through grace. "Let them all sign themselves with the sign of the cross of Christ; let them all respond Amen; let them all sing Allelluia. . . . Those that have charity are born of God; those that have it not, are not born of God: A mighty token, a mighty distinction! Have what you will; if this alone you have not, it profits you nothing: other things if you have not, have this, and you have fulfilled the law."[96]

God has done it all! It is in gratitude that the believer lives. The mind as God's creation is endowed with a natural capacity for remembering, understanding, and willing of itself; and when these powers are rightly directed, the true self will be recognized in its true order of being, in relation to the God whose image it is. In man's fallen condition, sin holds this natural capacity in abeyance, but can never completely destroy it: here the working of grace is seen. Grace awakens the dormant power in man to see God's image in himself—to see himself in God's image. This discovery of the likeness, now obscured by sin, the recovery of the Divine image, only takes effect in and through the influence of grace.

> The grace of God through Jesus Christ Our Lord must be understood as that by which alone men are delivered from evil, and without which they do absolutely no good thing, whether in thought, or will and affection, or in deed; not only in order that they may know by the manifestation of the same what should be done, but moreover in order that by its enabling they may do with love what they know.[97]

Once Pelagius and Caelestius were disposed of, it might be expected that Augustine would have a change of pace; he deserved some respite. It did not come. "Who does not weep on this rough road of ours here, when the very baby begins it with weeping? . . . And men laugh and men weep; and what we men laugh at is to be wept at."[98]

Julian of Eclanum

Pelagius had a new adherent in the recently elevated bishop of Eclanum, Julian. Son and son-in-law of bishops, Julian had wealth and status. He was a charming, resourceful, and powerful opponent who relentlessly defied Augustine during the concluding years of the man's life. *The African* was the designation Julian always used for Augustine. From 419 onward, Julian wrote, preached, and mustered all possible opposition against Augustine.

Pelagianism had been safely condemned by both Pope and Emperor as rank heresy. Julian was therefore most circumspect as to the method whereby he resurrected various inculcations, and he always did so from some distant land. In 418 Julian, aged thirty-five, led some Italian bishops in a resistance. He was forced to flee to Greece where the cele-

brated Theodore of Mopsuestia welcomed him in Cilicia. He then
moved on to Constantinople. He attempted a return to Italy to be rein-
stated, but the effort failed. He was a superb biblical scholar, and made
fun of the now deceased Jerome. He wrote with a facile pen, and refused to be silent.

So it was that a tired man in mid-sixties attacked with *Against Julian and the Pelagians*:

> Know . . . that good will, that good work, without the grace of
> God which is given through the one Mediator of God and man,
> can be granted to no one; and by this alone can man be brought
> to the eternal gift and kingdom of God. As to all other things,
> therefore, which among men seem to have some praise due
> them, . . . this I know, so far as I am concerned, that good will
> does not do them, for an unbelieving and impious will is not
> good.[99]

In assailing Julian, Augustine reveals a great deal of his own spiritual peregrination. For almost forty years he had lived as a faithful Servant of God and he had gained immeasurably. "For, no one is known
to another as he is to himself, yet neither is he so well known to himself as to be sure of his place of abode tomorrow."[100] At one time, at
the beginning of ministry, he had a happy, almost ingenuous quality in
his view toward humanity; goodness of individuals was almost assumed. Now, with his age and experience he questioned: Could human
nature really be trusted? "When I was writing this we were told that a
man of eighty-four, who had lived a life of continence under religious
observance with a pious wife for twenty-five years, had gone and
bought himself a music-girl for his pleasure." If angels were left to
their own free will they might lapse.[101] He was seeing the weakness of
human nature, and the limitations of man. What was the inevitable out-
come? Election by God. As man became increasingly entrapped in his
own sin, so Augustine prayerfully reasoned, here more and more the
initiative for goodness and for salvation itself, resided with God alone.
The concept of divine decree was becoming firmly established, "an un-
shakeable number of the elect" as the sons of God were "permanently
inscribed in the archives of the Father."[102] One cannot with impunity
question the Almighty!

Augustine insisted this doctrine had always been proclaimed by the church. Cyprian had presented the church as gathered saints whom God alone could enable to survive the bitter hostility of the world. It was a matter of how man was to survive. Survival of the Catholic Church was guaranteed, and this came through the "predestinate plan of God" for the elect. It was a somber view but, for Augustine, it was the only answer to the precarious notion of man's innate goodness and his freedom to do as he wills.

And what of God's justice? Said Augustine:

> He who lives according to the justice which is in the law, without the faith of the grace of Christ, . . . must be accounted to have no true justice; not because the law is not true and holy, but because to wish to obey the letter which commands without the quickening Spirit of God, as if by the strength of free will, is not true justice.[103]

He makes an analogy: "You have two servants, one deformed in person, the other very beautiful. . . . You have questioned the eyes of the flesh, and what report have they brought back to you? . . . Weigh justice and iniquity together. . . . Give me beauteous justice, give me the beauty of faith. . . . In each step prove yourselves lovers of justice."[104] For Augustine there is something basically unfair in Pelagianism: man is not able to bring about justice in his own strength. "From the very beginning of the human race no one passes to death but through Adam, and no one through Adam but passes to death; and no one attains to life but through Christ, and no one through Christ but attains to life. . . . For if some are saved without Christ, and some justified without Christ, then Christ died to no purpose."[105]

While Augustine was ruthless as an adversary, he was also a man of great tenderness. "My dear son, Julian," he began:

> I hope, with the help of the Lord . . . to make you understand, if that be possible, how fortunate it is for you to believe what you seek to convince others of. I hope also to inspire you with a salutary repentance of the errors to which the temerity of your youth and imprudence have led you.

> I have not forgotten your father, Memorius, of blessed memory, with whom I was united by a close friendship through letters. It was he that inspired me with a tenderness for you.

As for me, in virtue of the tenderness I have for you and which, with the grace of God, no insult will ever tear from my heart, I wish ardently, Julian, my dearest son, that by a better and stronger youth, you will triumph over yourself and that a sincere and true piety will make you renounce your ambitions and completely human desire which leads you to insist upon your own opinion, whatever it be, precisely because it is your opinion. . . . If the counsel I give you displeases you, act as you see fit. If you agree to correct yourself, as I most ardently wish, I will be filled with joy. If on the contrary . . . you persist in your error, I hope to draw profit from the reproaches you inflict upon me, for they will augument the reward that I await in heaven. In making my sorrow because of you more bitter, they will give me the opportunity to exercise mercy.[106]

Julian died in Sicily, a defeated, lonely pariah, but always claiming to be a good Catholic. He had made one strategic, and colossal, blunder: he attempted to lock horns with Augustine.

Augustine felt he was led of God to champion the Church and keep her doctrine pure. It was Easter, and he was preaching on "Cast the nets on the right side." Nets—a splendid symbol:

Furthermore, it was also stated that the nets were broken. When nets have been borken, heresies and schisms have taken place. The nets, indeed, take in all persons; but unmanageable fishes, those who do not wish to come to the food of the Lord, push, break out, and leave whenever they can. To be sure, the nets are stretched out over the whole world; those who break out, however, do so in certain places. The Donatists broke away in Africa, the Arians broke away in Egypt, the Photinians broke away in Pannonia, the Cataphrygians broke away in Phrygia, and the Manichaeans in Persia. In how many places the net has been broken![107]

Indeed, nets had broken in many places, and like James and John, he was mending by the side of the sea.

The First Puritan

Augustine was a puritan, perhaps the first in a distinguished succession of dedicated, highly sensitive individuals who, in total commitment to Christ, thrust all else aside. It was a reckless abandon for the cause which surmounted and surpassed all others. Nothing else dare stand in the way of righteousness. No personal relationships, no private feelings, no individual desires could be permitted to thwart the intent of doing God's will. Sinful pleasures were to be extirpated.

Time and events had wrought an Augustine who was the strict, moral, demanding puritan. It was, in part, reaction to the life he had once lived; the pendulum was now swinging as far to the right as it had once swung to the left. Augustine the profligate had become Augustine the seer. He who once reveled lasciviously now drove his mind and soul in constant devotion to the God who had mercifully saved him. Far from attempting to expiate for past sins—Christ had done that on the Cross—it was now Augustine's endeavor to express gratitude for the faith so clear and real. Thus when Truth is present, error cannot be tolerated. Compromise with falsehood, the devil, sin, or lubricous indulgence would betray a sacred trust. There can be no middle ground: right is right, wrong is wrong! Moral fiber becomes a major element in the Christian's makeup. Painful discipline is good for the soul. "On the timbrel leather is stretched, on the psaltery strings of cat gut, on either instrument the flesh is crucified. . . . The more the strings are stretched the higher in the scale they sound. . . . Christ touched them, and the sweetness of truth rang out."[108]

Beginning with his personal life—conduct in all matters—and then moving into the community of the faithful in Christ's Church, and thence into the world, Augustine stood as the strict Christian moralist. Uprightness of life was an absolute, a stern, unrelenting submission to the demands of the gospel—made possible for the believer by God's grace. For Augustine it had been a titanic struggle against the evil in his past. In remembering these past iniquities he now emphasised his, and man's, moral responsibility to a God of Righteousness, whose glory it was a redeemed sinner's chief duty to promote. Purity of character, personal discipline, a never-ending sense of humility, therefore, make the Christian a more effective servant of God. All the while, in the midst of making somber judgment on sins personal and communal, there must be adoration. "Even when one confesses his sins, he ought to do so with praise of God; nor is a confession of sins a pious one unless it be made without despair, and with a prayer for God's mercy."[109]

From the personal, Augustine transferred his moral code to the larger stage, the community, the state.

> Where is the Christian to live apart, that he may not groan among false brethren? Whither is he to go? What is he to do? Is he to seek solitudes?. . . Because you seem to have had speedy feet in passing over, will you cut off the bridge? . . . I will live apart with a few good men, said some one. With them it will be well with me. For to do good to no man is wicked and cruel. . . . I will not admit any wicked man, any wicked brother to my society. With a few good men it will be well with me. How do you recognise the person whom perhaps it is your wish to exclude? That he may be known to be wicked, he must be tested within; how then do you shut out one about to enter, who must be proved afterwards, and who cannot be proved unless he has entered? Will you repel all the wicked?. . . For we all wish to have our hearts fortified, that no evil suggestion may enter. But who knows whence it enters? Every day, even, we fight within our own heart. Within his own heart one man is at strife with a multitude. Avarice suggests, lust suggests, gluttony suggests, popular rejoicing suggests, all things suggest. . . . Where then is security? Here nowhere, in this life nowhere, except solely in God's promise. But there, when we shall have attained thereto, is perfect security; when the gates of Jerusalem are shut and the bolts of her gates strengthened.[110]

Christian morality not only means rejection of evil, it means avid engagement in doing good.

So Augustine thought of society, and he thought of it terms of morality, uprightness and goodness, hard work and careful saving of the fruits of labor. It is the puritan ideal, for Augustine is a puritan. As he moved into consideration of the role and function of the state, he did so with a puritan's critical eye. Society stands under the judgment of the Almighty. The state cannot violate the moral laws of God with impunity. Augustine's philosophy of history was aborning. It was a strict puritan view. "We are Christians, we belong to Christ."[111]

X

Search for a City
A.D. 410

During the turbulent years just before and after A.D. 410 the Christians of Africa experienced something hitherto unknown—a gnawing anxiety. It had been so obvious, in previous years that the Catholic Church was growing; and Augustine reflected the mood. Now there were shocking reverses: "We all know why those who at all fear God defer their conversions; it is because they hope for a longer life." The bishop continued, "Tomorrow, tomorrow is the ruin of many, for they will suddenly find the door closed."[1] There had been good times, now there were unparalleled disasters.[2] A great many faithful Catholics were wondering why Africa should not return to the old days, bring back long gone pagan institutions—circuses, games. It was at least an outward show of glory, a reminder that the state was intact, and a fleeting escape from funereal reality. Augustine sensed the impending doom that gripped his people; he likewise appreciated the utter futility of restored circuses and histrionics. "Many sinful and abandoned men so train their bodies that, by diverse arts, they can perform such remarkable feats . . . [as] rope dancers and other theatrical performers."[3] It had to be far deeper.

What could he do for his people and what must he do within himself? He began, at this critical juncture, by preaching masterful sermons, addressing himself to the needs of his African people. And what was their need? A sense of belonging. They were Christians, but all about them were pagans. They were thus a distinct race, a holy nation of "citizens of Jerusalem." He turned to his Psalms—he had always loved them. Here he found magnificent figures of speech "which everyone brought up in the traditions of the holy church should know."[4] He looked out at his congregation and cried, "O God's own people, O Body of Christ, O high-born race of foreigners on earth . . . you do not belong here, you belong somewhere else."[5]

Augustine began his major thesis: since Adam's fall, humanity has been divided into two great cities (he has not forgotten his Plato). One "city" serves God and the loyal angels. The other "city" is ruled by the devil and his rebel angels and demons. At the Last Judgment the two cities will be separated—presently they appear "inextricably mixed"—and they will be clearly seen as Jerusalem and Babylon.[6] It is the Matthew 25:31-46 passage, with the sheep and goats. He likewise talked about the wheat and the tares.

While the Jews were in bondage in Babylon they longed for their Jerusalem, and prophets proclaimed a return, and all looked to the native city. Augustine portrayed it dramatically to his African people: captivity and liberation, loss and reparation:

> We also must know first our captivity, then our liberation: we must know Babylon and Jerusalem. . . . There two cities, as a matter of historical fact, were two cities recorded in the Bible. . . . They were founded, at precise moments, to crystallize in symbolic form, the reality of those two "cities" that had begun in the remote past, and that will continue to the end of the world.[7]

Jews, observed Augustine, had trudged obediently to Babylon and served as loyal public servants. Lo, their prayers were answered in the conversion of King Nebuchadnezzar. These Jews may have been physically in Babylon, yet they were never part of it. Through ordeal of captivity they learned their true citizenship—Jerusalem; and they would someday return.[8] "Now let us hear, brothers, let us hear and sing; let us pine for the City where we are citizens. . . . By pining, we are already there; we have already cast our hope, like an anchor, on that coast. I sing of somewhere else, not of here: for I sing with my heart, not my flesh. The citizens of Babylon hear the sound of the flesh, the Founder of Jerusalem hears the tune of our heart."[9]

Many moralists, Pelagius in particular, placed heavy emphasis on the Judgment, a time fast approaching. Augustine's view was that of a judgment—but it was a softer note. It was future, and to be anticipated with joy for that immemorial country. "Was it in order to have a prosperous time in this world that you became a Christian?" he asked. "Are you in torments at seeing the wicked flourish here and now, when hereafter they will suffer torments with the devil for company? Why such complaint? Why are you fainthearted because of the waves and storms on the lake? Why?" The answer is clear:

> Because Jesus is asleep, or rather your faith which comes from Jesus has fallen asleep in your heart. . . . Our Lord will awake; in other words, your faith will return to you, and with His help you will see in your soul that the gift given today to the wicked will not be theirs forever. . . . As for the gift held in pledge for you, it will be yours for all eternity. . . . Turn your back, then, on all that falls away, and your face toward all that is eternal.[10]

Augustine had implicit faith in the God of History, the vast sweep of the ages. He had discovered part of the secret when he first plunged into Genesis—the orderly process of creation. God had a plan for it all.

> Does not summer follow winter, with a gradual increase of heat? Childhood, never to return, gives place to youth; vigorous manhood, doomed not to last, succeeds to youth; old age, putting an end to vigorous manhood, is itself ended by death. All these are changes, yet the method of Divine Providence by which they are made to change does not change.[11]

In like fashion, changes come in religious institutions, and Israel is a splendid example of becoming. The human race is like "one vast organism," a single man: "The experience of mankind in general, as far as God's people is concerned, is comparable to the experience of the individual man. There is a process of education, through the epochs of a peoples' history, as through the successive stages of a man's life."[12]

For Augustine, history was filled with meaning, for all time is vested in God's hands and his purposes. Therefore, in the face of stark tragedy, the Christian community of Africa can be filled with hope:

> Being the unchangeable Creator as well as Ruler of the world of change, He knows as well what and when to give, to add to, to take away, to withdraw, to increase, or to diminish, until the

> beauty of the entire world, of which the individual parts are
> suitable each for its own time, swells, as it were, into a mighty
> song of some unutterable musician, and from thence the true
> adorers of God rise to the eternal contemplation of His face,
> even in the time of faith.[13]

Humanity—in Christ—is in process of developing.

"For a man is never in so good a state as when his whole life is a
journey towards the immutable life, and his affections are entirely set
upon it," wrote Augustine. "If, however, he loves himself for his own
sake, he does not look at himself in relation to God, but turns his mind
in upon himself, and so is not occupied with anything that is immutable."[14] Only as men and nations relate to God is there any meaning
whatsoever in life. Apart from God, men and nations know only vanity
and—eventually—oblivion.

> What are we to say, brethren, in the face of the sufferings our
> enemies have inflicted upon Christians, and of their delirious
> joy in their victory? And when will it be made obvious that
> their victory is illusory? When these are covered with confusion
> and the others with joy at the advent of the Lord our God, who
> will come bearing in His hand each one's recompense; to the
> reprobate, damnation; to the just, a kingdom; to the evildoers,
> fellowship with the devil; to the faithful, fellowship with
> Christ.[15]

Augustine the preacher looked at his congregation. "Now therefore, my brethren, let us sing, not for our delight as we rest, but to
cheer us in our labour. As wayfarers are wont to sing, sing, but keep on
marching.... If you are progressing, you are marching; but progress in
good, progress in the true faith, progress in right living; sing, and
march on."[16]

City of God A.D. 410–426

"The whole question, which troubles active and inquiring persons,
such as I am, is this: how to live among people or near people who
have not yet learned to live by dying, not by a fleshly dissolution, but
by deliberately turning the mind away from the enticements of the
flesh." He now saw it, and he saw it with clarity: "Thus we are
dragged down by these dusty and earthy desires, and we have a hard

time lifting up our sluggish hearts to God.''[17] Augustine was convinced that a Christian must live out a life of faithful discipleship among people—not the recluse. And this life was to be lived with an eye to another city:

> I realize that I am in dangerous straits in so many matters, and especially in those which I have referred to as briefly as I could. All this ignorance and difficulty seem to me to arise from the fact that we administer the government not of an earthly and Roman people, but of the heavenly Jerusalem.[18]

Africa had long made a point of the Heavenly Jerusalem. Paganism was everywhere, but the Christian lived above it—or he *ought* to. Augustine's people were Roman, they were African, they were also of another clime, another land. They were moving to that city which Abraham had envisioned and John had seen. And now, the crosscurrents of history were moving into juxtaposition with Augustine's philosophy of the human endeavor. Rome was falling.

Events in the Roman world were now moving at accelerated speed. Decline, in spite of the protestations of some intellectuals, was a grim reality. The day of doom arrived. On August 24, 410, a Gothic army, led by Alaric, entered the Eternal City. His nickname, "the Daring," was appropriate. Born in 370 at the mouth of the Danube, son of a great Visigoth family, he had lived most of his life within the boundaries of the empire and he regarded himself as its defender. He wanted imperial recognition: pensions for his men and a post in the high command at Rome. If his demands had been met he probably would have spared the city. The languid Emperor and his indecisive Imperial Court might have averted the tragedy, but, as usual, they failed to muster sufficient courage, resolution, and political deftness to meet the crisis. As it was, for three days there was general looting and parts of the city were burned. During two previous years the Goths had besieged the city, "starving the inhabitants into cannibalism," but there had not been an invasion. Now the streets of the city resounded with the dull tread of a conquering horde. Pelagius had seen it:

> It happened only recently, and you heard it yourself. Rome, the mistress of the world, shivered, crushed with fear, at the sound of the blaring trumpets and the howling of the Goths. Where, then, was the Nobility? Where were the certain and distinct

ranks of dignity? Everyone was mingled together and shaken with fear; every household had its grief and an all pervading terror gripped us. Slave and noble were one. The same spectre of death stalked before us all.[19]

Rome had ceased to be the political capital of the empire years earlier, but the city remained as symbol of Western culture, an entire civilization. It likewise represented guarantee of—outward—tranquility. "If Rome can perish," wailed Jerome from Bethlehem, "what can be safe?"[20]

A great many wealthy Romans had vast estates in Africa, and hither they rushed, in tears. From these distraught refugees Augustine gained a firsthand account of the disaster:

All the devastation, the butchery, the plundering, the conflagrations, and all the anguish which accompanied the recent disaster at Rome were in accordance with the general practice of warfare. But there was something which established a new custom, something which changed the whole aspect of the scene; the savagery of the barbarians took on such an aspect of gentleness that the largest basilicas were selected and set aside to be filled with people to be spared by the enemy.[21]

He listened thoughtfully, made his plans, brought his sense of history into focus, but, above all, he coalesced his tremendous theological understanding and acumen. Writing in 427, he told how he envisioned his answer to the fall of Rome:

Meanwhile, Rome was destroyed as a result of an invasion of the Goths under the leadership of King Alaric, and of the violence of this great disaster. The worshipers of the many false gods, whom we call by the customary name pagans, attempting to attribute its destruction to the Christian religion, began to blaspheme the true God more sharply and bitterly than usual. And so, "burning with zeal for the house of God," I decided to write the books, *On the City of God*, in opposition to their blasphemies and errors. This work kept me busy for some years. . . . But finally, this extensive work . . . was completed in twenty-two books.[22]

Life had been preparing Augustine for this particular moment. He would say that God was responsible for those personal experiences into the vortex of which he had been hurled, and out of it he learned, grew, deepened. He wrote to Marcellinus, "Thanks to the Lord our God, who has sent us a sovereign help against those evils! Where would that stream of the repulsive malice of the human race not have carried us, who would not have been swept along with it, in what depths would it not have overwhelmed us, if the cross of Christ had not been planted, firm and high, in the great rock of authority, so that we might take hold of its strength and be steadied, and might not be drawn under the vast current of the ruined world by listening to evil advisers, urging us to evil."[23]

The *City of God* stands as one of the epochal works in Western culture. Only a genius could have produced it, "the last great apology of the church against paganism, the final justification of her teaching and historical position at the end of time, and before the whole world."[24] Augustine refused to panic. For years he had looked, not to Rome, but to Ravenna as source of Roman authority, for here resided Honorius the Emperor, that "pale flower of the women's quarters"[25] who persisted in issuing decrees written in gold on purple stationery. Augustine was quite loyal; in fact, he turned to Theodosius the Great—father of Honorius—as the model Christian prince.

Perhaps Augustine remembered too well his own unhappy days in Rome to have any romantic notion about the city. For him and his fellow African bishops, it was certainly less than the great African municipalities of Carthage and Alexandria and the Eastern capital Constantinople. The true Christian community looked to centers where pagan influence had been purged. "Pottery is hardened by fire; so the strength of Christ's Body is not consumed by fire like straw, but hardened, like pottery, by the fire of His Passion."[26] Really, pagan Rome received her just deserts. She had brought it on herself. Augustine thought in terms of the Christian Imperial Court which had resided safely in Ravenna as center of authority rather than the old city by the Tiber. He knew the hoary empire was no more. Britain was virtually independent, Gaul irreclaimably lost, the East—from Greece to Mesopotamia—completely separate. Where, then, was the real power in Augustine's world: the Catholic Church. Here was the one hope for humanity. In the Church there was unity, and here was the locus of power. Thus his rationale for *City of God:*

The first five of these books refute those persons who would so view the prosperity of human affairs that they think that the worship of the many gods whom the pagans worship is necessary for this; they contend that these evils arise and abound because they are prohibited from doing so. The next five books, however, speak against those who admit that these evils have never been wanting and never will be wanting to mortals, and that these, at one time great, at another time slight, vary according to place, times, and persons; and yet they argue that the worship of many gods, whereby sacrifice is offered to them, is useful because of the life to come after death. In these ten books, then, these two false beliefs, contrary to the Christian religion, are refuted.[27]

It was an arduous undertaking, even for Augustine, who was now in his sixtieth year. He began in early 413 and by the next year had completed the first three books. The fourth was finished by the end of 415. By 416 he had brought to completion books five to eleven. The next three books engaged his time until 420, and the last eight books were written between 420 and the spring of 426. Augustine published the books at intervals, and finally touched up the entire work before he sent it to the African priest Firmus instructing him that he had re-read, and in places probably emended,[28] the whole *magnum opus*.

"I have taken upon myself the task of defending the glorious City of God against those who prefer their own gods to the Founder of that City," said the author to Marcellinus in his prefatory letter. His introduction illustrates exactly what Augustine had in mind, for this was the illustrious Marcellinus sent by the emperor to preside at the Council of Carthage. Marcellinus was eager to convert Volusianus, Proconsul of Africa, a noble only mildly interested in Christianity. He also objected to the undermining of the old Roman ideas—this had brought about the fall. It was in answer to the charge that neglect of pagan virtues, ideals, and deities brought collapse that the Bishop of Hippo wrote, "From this world's city there arise enemies against whom the City of God has to be defended."Who are the real enemies of Rome? Pagans.

> I classify the human race into two branches: the one consists of those who live by human standards, the other of those who live according to God's will. . . . By two cities I mean two societies

of human beings, one of which is predestined to reign with God from all eternity, the other doomed to undergo eternal punishment with the Devil.[29]

Is the City of God the Church? It is more than an institution, "Now the philosophers against whose attacks we are defending the City of God, that is to say, God's Church . . ."[30] is but a single reference. Of far greater significance is the identification with the "People of God" from Adam to Christ, and following the Resurrection, those who believe in Christ. His view of the institutional church is made specific: a visible body, governed by bishops who are the successors of the apostles, and the bishop of Rome—the apostolic see—can speak for the entire church. But he does not dwell on the point, rather moving from the institution to the "supernatural reality of the congregation of the predestined" who are in divine mission:

> In the same way, while the City of God is on pilgrimage in this world, she has in her midst some who are united with her in participation in the sacraments, but who will not join with her in the eternal destiny of the saints. Some of these are hidden; some are well known, for they do not hesitate to murmur against God, whose sacramental signs they bear, even in the company of his acknowledged enemies. At one time they join his enemies in filling the theatres, at another they join with us in filling the churches.[31]

Presumably these enemies will eventually be converted. Too, there are those of the old dispensation, and what better example than "Job, that holy and amazing man. He was neither a native of Israel nor a proselyte . . . such is the praise accorded him in inspired utterances that no man of his period is put on the same level as far as righteousness and devotion are concerned."[32]

Augustine made great use of the "consequences of sin" as the basis for much of man's condition, and slavery is an example: "For it is understood, of course, that the condition of slavery is justly imposed on the sinner. That is why we do not hear of a slave anywhere in the Scriptures until Noah, the just man, punished his son's sin with this word; and so that son deserved this name because of his misdeed, not because of his nature."[33] Slavery in Augustine's day was economic. Slaves were taken as booty in war. It was not racial; there were perhaps more white than black slaves. The punitive character of slavery resulted from sin. He admits the institution is contrary to basic equality of all men as human beings. Prior to entering Augustine's monastery, a deacon had purchased several slaves. When Augustine learned of it he said to the entire fellowship, "This deacon must free those slaves today in your presence before being allowed to join you."[34] Yet the fact remains—human sinfulness is the root problem, thus coercion is accepted as a result. In writing to Largus, Proconsul in Africa, Augustine comments:

> In this world it is impossible not to fear, not to grieve, not to labor, not to be in danger, but it is a matter of utmost importance for what reason, with what hope, for what purpose a man suffers those trials. As for me, when I look at the lovers of this world, I do not know when wisdom has the best opportunity of healing their souls. But they enjoy apparent prosperity, they scornfully reject her wholesome warnings and esteem them as an old wives' ditty; when they are pinched by adversity, they are more intent on escaping the source of their present straits than on laying hold of what may furnish a cure and a place of refuge from which anguish is completely excluded. . . . I do not wish you to suffer hereafter such trials as you have already endured, I wish still more that you may not have endured them without some change for the better in your life.[35]

Suffering is part of man's plight, and sin brings immeasurable agony.

Augustine's view of the state, a commonwealth, "we must ascribe to the true God alone the power to grant kingdoms and empires. [He] grants earthly kingdoms both to the good and to the evil, in accordance with his pleasure, which can never be unjust. . . . The same God gave power to Marius and to Gaius Caesar, to Augustus and to Nero . . . the most attractive emperors, as well as . . . the most ruthless tyrant; . . . to Constantine the Christian, and also to Julian the Apostate." He summed it up: "It is clear that God, the one true God, rules and guides these events, according to his pleasure. If God's reasons are inscrutable, does that mean that they are unjust?"[36] No! His ways are beyond human understanding.

As he makes his way through the *City of God*, Augustine finds delectation in his philosophy, which he cannot forget, and at the same time he turns upon the philosophers with fierceness: "But the Platonists have not been able to play the part of true reason as fully as the others. . . . For, all of them lacked the model of divine humility . . . our Lord Jesus Christ."[37] He charges Porphyry, "For all this, . . . you acknowledge the existence of grace, when you say that it is granted only to few to reach God by virtue of their intelligence. . . . You even use the word 'grace' itself quite openly in the passage where, following Plato, you assert without hesitation that man cannot by any means reach the perfection of wisdom in this life, but that, after this life, all those who live the life of the intellect receive all that is needed for their fulfillment from the providence and the grace of God." He then makes his supreme plea to ancient philosophy; his very being cries out to those giants of human thought who will always be dear to him:

> If only you had recognized the grace of God through Jesus Christ our Lord! If only you had been able to see his incarnation, in which he took a human soul and body, as the supreme instance of grace! But what can I do? I know that it is to no avail that I speak to a dead man. . . . But there are people who hold you in high regard, who are attached to you . . . they are the audience to whom my colloquy is really directed, and it may be that for them it is not in vain.[38]

What of paganism? "Someone will ask, 'Do you yourself believe those tales?' No, I certainly do not believe them; and Varro, the most learned of the Romans, almost admits their falsity, though timidly and diffidently. But he asserts that it is an advantage to communities that brave men should believe themselves to be sons of gods, even if it is not true." He turns back to Rome of the seventh century B.C. in the war on Alba, "and the third abode of the Trojan gods, was overthrown. . . . A striking sign of this disastrous state of things was the fact that none of those kings closed the Gates of War. That shows that none of them reigned in peace, though they were under the protection of all those gods."[39] Augustine was saying to the Roman world: what a farce all this has been, and you have not been able to see it.

It is specifically at this juncture that Augustine displays consummate skill as a writer, revealing a piercing, scathing wit. The most ludicrous—and rotten—aspect of Roman civilization was the debased admixture of cultism and sex. We can almost see the old man writing, an impish gleam in his eye, as he recalls the ribald stories, theatrics, inscriptions and statues in pagan Carthage and Rome. At last he could

—for the glory of God—weave in these scabrous legends which once enthralled him. Now those heinous sins could be put to good use: to reveal to the world the putrid nature of Roman life. To fortify his position, Augustine cites Varro to substantiate the tales.

Augustine graphically describes the modest Roman matrons having to divert their eyes to avoid the "indecent postures of the actors," yet these same women "by furtive glances" made themselves familiar with the techniques of vice. He describes, in Book VII, the obscene rites of the god Liber, in which the male organ of copulation is made the object of veneration. An enormous penis, painstakingly carved, would be placed on a cart and taken from town to town as a traveling exhibition of worship. As the supreme insult to respectability, the most esteemed mother of the community was compelled to make public display by placing garlands on the carved genital.

It was the revolting notion of multiplicity of gods and their sex functions, graphically described in Book VI, that becomes Augustine's supreme disclosure of Roman decadence. With angry repartee he describes the marriage, and the utilities of the gods. The bridal chamber is so crowded with deities that Augustine marvels that the newlyweds are not embarrassed. There are sexual functions and gods aplenty to oversee every act. Subigus will subdue, and Prema is to press. There is Pertunda, to pierce, in case the new husband needs divine assistance. Finally Augustine is forced to observe, "Let the bridegroom have something to do for himself." Priapus is on hand, "and the newly wedded bride used to be told to sit on his phallus." It was all "monstrous obscenity" but Romans blithely regarded it as the most honorable and religious of actions. Disgusting! Let this Rome perish in its own poisonous sewage.

In contrast to this filth Augustine points with joyous pride to the wholesomeness of the Christian faith. Christ brings simplicity and purity into life. There is moral goodness, health, and felicity. The Christian culture was able to enhance the good in Roman tradition, and refine, redeem the bad, removing the dross, cleansing the impurities in the fire of God's truth.

Rome had a glorious past, and how did it come about, "Let us go on to examine for what moral qualities and for what reason the true God deigned to help the Romans in the extension of their empire; for in his control are all the kingdoms of the earth."And why, then, did it all come to an end?

> They were passionately devoted to glory; it was for this that they desired to live, for this they did not hesitate to die. This unbounded passion for glory, above all else, checked their other appetites. They felt it would be shameful for their country to be enslaved, but glorious for her to have dominion and empire; and so they set their hearts first on making her free, then on making her sovereign.[40]

Augustine gave the world his philosophy of history. He brought the fruit of a lifetime of thought, and lovingly presented it to God. The work is his commentary on two cultures, pagan and Christian, on evil and good.

In Carthage, Augustine was preaching, "When, therefore, death shall be swallowed up in victory, these things will not be there; and there shall be peace—peace full and eternal. We shall be in a kind of city. Brethren, when I speak of that City, and especially when scandals grow great here, I just cannot bring myself to stop."[41] So he labored on his "great and arduous work" and in so doing provided a classic which future generations would grapple with. "There we shall be still and see; we shall see and we shall love; we shall love and we shall praise. Behold what will be, in the end, without end! For what is our end but to reach that kingdom which has no end?"

As Augustine brought his masterpiece to a close, he gave a synopsis of last things: "For the first immortality, which Adam lost by sinning, was the ability to avoid death; the final immortality will be the inability to die." He continued:

> By sinning we lose our hold on piety and happiness; and yet in losing our happiness we do not lose the will to happiness. Certainly God himself cannot sin; are we therefore to say that God has no free will?
>
> In the Heavenly City then, there will be freedom of will. It will be one and the same freedom in all, and indivisible in the separate individuals. It will be freed from all evil and filled with all good, enjoying unfailingly the delight of eternal joys, forgetting all offences, forgetting all punishments. Yet it will not forget its own liberation, nor be ungrateful to its liberator. It will remember even its past evils as far as intellectual knowledge is

concerned; but it will utterly forget them as far as sense experience is concerned.

So Augustine closes, "And now, as I think, I have discharged my debt, with the completion, by God's help, of this huge work. It may be too much for some, too little for others. . . . I make this request: that they do not thank me, but join with me in rendering thanks to God. Amen. Amen."[42]

XI

Faithful in Administration
A.D. 410–420

"When I picture a bishop, straitened and harried on all sides by the clamorous cares of the Church."[1] Augustine was writing a personal letter, but more, he was expressing his existential situation. It was a life of important drudgery. There were, among other demands, annual councils in Carthage. The fifteenth Council of Carthage convened in early 410 and, despite his loathing of travel, Augustine was in attendance. His presence was essential: he was spokesman for the bishops. Though they often disagreed, they looked to him. He was not in good health; meetings fatigued him. Upon returning to Hippo he retired to a villa outside the city and remained there for the duration of the winter. He shuddered at the penetrating cold of winter. Even in semi-seclusion, as soon as warm months approached, writings appeared. His *Letter to Dioscorus* was followed by *On Single Baptism.* The year 411 saw that fierce engagement with the Donatists who had come to Carthage for the Council. Augustine preached at Carthage regularly, from January to March, and at Cirta as well as at Carthage from April to June—all against the Donatists. It was exhausting. He poured out his feelings to Honoratus, a catechumen: "When, then, our prayers are not heard in regard to keeping or gaining temporal goods, when we ask God for these, inasmuch as He does not hear us, He forsakes us, but, in regard to the better gifts which He wishes us to understand and prefer and desire, He does not forsake us."[2]

During these years when so many refugees were fleeing to Africa, Augustine encountered an illustrious Roman family, recently arrived at their estate in Hippo. The situation is farcical. Pinianus came with his wife Melania and mother Albina. They were of tremendous wealth and known everywhere for their piety and great generosity. Immediately the people of Hippo hit upon the happy idea of making full use of Pinianus as a patron who could easily provide all the money the church needed. Their misguided zeal proved to be an embarrassment to Augustine, and a terror to the visitors. On his first visit to the Basilica, Pinianus was seized bodily as the congregation, with terrifying persistent shouting"[3] demanded that he remain in the city as their priest (a manner not unlike that to which Augustine had been subjected). Pinianus was actually held for hours while letters were exchanged, and offers and counter offers were made. At last the distinguished visitors were able to disentangle themselves physically and, once away from the building, they fled from the city, shocked at such turbulence. Letters followed from Augustine offering apology for the scene. "The people of Hippo, to whom the Lord has given me as servant," he wrote, "and who are weakened to such a great and almost universal extent that the onset of even a slight trouble could put them into a serious illness, are now stricken with so grave a trouble that, even if they were not so weak, they could scarcely meet it with any health of mind."[4]

To add to already burdensome tasks, Augustine received a long communication from Marcellinus, late in 411, telling him that Pelagianism was spreading in Carthage. In response, Augustine preached a series of messages, *Sermons against the Pelagians*. He also took time to write his *Discourse on Peace* and his *Treatise on the Punishment and Remission of Sin*.

As he was being sucked into the midst of the political, ecclesiastical maelstrom, Augustine gasped a bit of humor, as in his letter to Jerome, suggesting the past be buried in oblivion: "Someone once fell into a well where the water was deep enough to hold him up so that he did not drown, but not enough to choke him so that he could not speak. A bystander came over when he saw him and asked sympathetically: 'How did you fall in?' He answered: 'Please find some way of getting me out and never mind how I fell in.' "[5] A bit of whimsey was needed occasionally to relieve the tedium and the tragedy. As the sage of Hippo meditated on Psalm 112 he concluded, "Let your old age be childlike, and your childhood like old age; that is, so that neither may your wisdom be with pride, nor your humility without wisdom."

Once more Augustine was in the pulpit at Carthage, September through December of 412, and he also wrote *On Correcting the Donatists*. He was at the same rostrum again in January of 413, and he was writing *Faith and Works*. These were grim days, and Augustine faced hectic and heartrending situations, as during the short-lived revolt of Heraclian, Count of Africa. Reprisals followed and, of all people, loyal Marcellinus was seized and given a sham of a trial. In attempting to aid his faithful friend, Augustine rushed back to Carthage in June and again in August and September. It was to no avail. Augustine was appalled. "It was the eve of the feast of blessed Cyprian" when this great and good Catholic, Marcellinus, was marched from his cell to the public garden. "It was not a place set apart for public execution, but a pleasure spot of the city."[6] There, on September 13, 413, Marcellinus was beheaded. Not only did Rome lose one of her most competent statesmen, but Augustine lost a dear friend. The Donatists, however, could rejoice. Grief is frequently assuaged by hard work, and at the end of the year Augustine completed *On Nature and Grace*.

The year 414 found the bishop in Hippo (his people did not want him to be away for too long a time) busy in preaching and writing. He concluded *On the Trinity* as well as *Homilies on the Gospel of John*. His extensive literary output continued unabated, with special attention to his commentaries. In September and October of 416 he attended the Council at Milevis, where Pelagius and Caelestius were condemned. The following year, 417, he began his lucid—and decimating— *Against Pelagius and Caelestius*. He was likewise writing his Letters to Boniface, Count of Africa—and a man of major significance. He preached in Carthage in September, and saw that his *On the Donatist Controversy* was circulated. "There is nothing in this life, and especially at this time, easier or more agreeable or more acceptable to men than the office of bishop or priest or deacon, if it is performed carelessly or in a manner to draw flattery;" lo, he does not stop, "but in God's sight there is nothing more wretched, more melancholy, or more worthy of punishment."[7]

The sixteenth Council of Carthage assembled in January of 418. Later that winter Augustine received a letter from Pinianus in Jerusalem, where he had just met Pelagius. Augustine fortified the noble Pinianus with a copy of *Against Pelagius and Caelestius*. In mid-year Augustine was at Caesarea in Mauretania and he published his *Discourse in Caesarea on Catholic Unity*.

In January of 419 the seventeenth Council of Carthage met in what had now become an annual assembly. Augustine had prompted the original idea when he first came to Hippo. The African bishops had an opportunity to discuss the affairs of the church but of greater import— to hear Augustine. His works included *On Marriage and Concupiscence*, *On the Origin of the Soul*, *Adulterous Marriages*, and treatises on biblical study.

Writings continued in 420, with *Against Julian and the Pelagians* and *Against Lying*. Toward the end of the year Augustine and Tribune Boniface met at Tubunae. It was an attempt on the bishop's part to secure Roman defense of Africa. Boniface's wife, a pious Catholic who had great influence on her husband, died in 420. The Count was distraught and even contemplated entering a monastery. Augustine's frantic visit was to appeal for armed might as a protection, and a Herculean effort to dissuade the Count against a hermit-like life. Africa needed him, not as a simple monk, but as a powerful general. Barbarian invasions were now a constant threat to Africa itself. How very interesting that the one who so zealously espoused the monastic ideal, should, in the face of ghastly reality, plead with a man to remain a soldier. Augustine was a realist and an engrossing pragmatist. He wrote:

> I praise and congratulate and admire you, my beloved son, Boniface, for your ardent desire to know the things that are of God, in the midst of the cares of war and arms. Indeed, it is clear that this is what makes you serve, with that same military valor, the faith which you have in Christ.[8]

Much later Augustine addressed another communication to Boniface; this time a sad rebuke, for Boniface had turned against the Emperor and formed a fatal alliance with the Vandals in Spain. It was an egregious error.

> Hear me, then, or, rather, hear the Lord our God speaking through me, His weak minister; recall what you were when your first wife of pious memory was still in the flesh and how, just after her death, you recoiled from the vanity of this world

and longed to enter the service of God. We know, we are wit-
nesses of what you said to us at Tubunae about your state of
mind and your intention. . . . You wanted, in fact, to give up all
the public business in which you were engaged, to retire into a
holy retreat and to live the life of a servant of God as the monks
live it. What kept you from doing it? Nothing but the thought,
urged by us, of the great benefit to the churches of Christ of
what you were doing, provided you did it with the sole intention of defending them from the incursions of barbarians.

While we were rejoicing over this proposal of yours, you sailed
away and you married a wife. . . . You would not have married
a wife if you had not been overcome by concupiscence and
given up the continence you had undertaken to keep. When I
heard it, I admit I was dumbfounded.

What shall I say of the many and great evils, matters of public
knowledge, which have resulted from your actions since your
marriage? You are a Christian, you have a conscience, you fear
God. Look into yourself and you will find what I shrink from
saying.[9]

Augustine saw that life made various demands of individuals. Situations were not always the same. A life of quiet contemplation was
greatly to be desired—by some pious souls in certain periods of history. The exigencies of the present African situation called for action.
A virulent and brutal enemy had to be vanquished; the homeland must
be safeguarded. No longer could there be languid security, the comfort
of feeling safe in their desert fastness.

Closing Years A.D. 421–430

Augustine's career continued at the same relentless pace, regardless
of age and physical health. Life refused to permit retirement. In 421 he
wearily journeyed to the eighteenth Council of Carthage. His writings
reflect the lingering conflict with the Pelagians: *Against Julian and the
Pelagians* as well as his sublime work on doctrine, *The Enchiridion,
Addresses to Laurentius, How to Help the Dead.* The following year,
422, found him at work on *The Eight Questions of Dulcitius* and, of
course, these months were spent on the perennial *City of God.*

Administrative requirements weighed heavily on the bishop's

shoulders, as in the humiliating affair of Antonius of Fussala. The village of Fussala was in Augustine's diocese. It was once a rabid stronghold of the Donatists. He found it necessary to deliver an unusually straightforward sermon on the duties of a bishop. Now he exercised his prerogative to choose a bishop for the community, but his first choice declined. He then presented and confirmed Antonius—a conniving autocrat who pigheadedly refused to resign even after he was found guilty of malfeasance. Augustine wrote at length to Pope Celestine, "I needed a man suitable and well adapted to that place, and one who was versed in the Punic language." Augustine woefully lamented the situation: "What am I to do?. . . . The case has reached such scandalous proportions that those who yielded to me in having him undertake the episcopacy, in the belief that it was to their own interest, and come to me and laid charges against him. Among these charges, the most serious crime, that of revolting immorality." The headstrong young Bishop Antonius took his case to Rome. African bishops were not of one mind. It was confusion compounded: the office of bishop was placed in a delicate posture. "His cry is: 'Either I ought to sit upon my own episcopal throne or I ought not to be a bishop,' as if he were now sitting on any throne but his own. It was for that reason that those districts in which he was first named bishop were set apart and entrusted to him, that he might not be said to have been transferred illegally to another's see, contrary to the decrees of the Fathers. But, should anyone be such a stickler for either severity or leniency as to inflict no punishment of any kind on men who do not seem to have deserved deprivation of their sees, or, on the other hand, to deprive those who seem to deserve some punishment of the honor of episcopacy?"[10]

Augustine's later years were not exclusively burdensome. He was enormously popular, and honors came to him, and there was joy, as in Jerome's letter of 418:

> Your fame is world-wide; Catholics revere you and accept you as the second founder of the ancient faith, and—which is a mark of greater fame—all the heretics hate you, and pursue me, too, with equal hatred; they plan our death by desire if they cannot achieve it by the sword.[11]

Then there were touching, personal encounters, as on one occasion when Augustine accepted a gift from a girl of Carthage, Sapida. She had made a tunic for her brother Timothy, a deacon, but he died before the gift was completed. She then presented it to the bishop: "I have received the work of your pious hands, which you wished me to have. . . I have accepted the tunic. . . . I had begun to wear it, before writing this letter."He concluded his piquant message with a reminder of her brother: "Be comforted that he is now clothed in the incorruption and immortality . . . having no further need for a corruptible garment."[12]

People took advantage of a kindly Augustine, as in the case of a sick man brought to him for healing. At first Augustine joked, "If I had the gift you say I have, I would be the first to try it on myself."[13] When told the man came as the result of a dream, the bishop complied, for Augustine set great store by dreams. It is somewhat ironic that in confrontations with Donatists, Augustine had spoken contemptuously of dreams as media of revelation—just as he had of miracles and relics. It was one thing to scoff at superstitious Donatists, but when Orosius returned from Jerusalem in 416 he brought to Africa relics of the recently discovered body of Stephen the Martyr. Within a year small chapels, claiming to possess a casket of holy dust, sprang up in many towns around Hippo. These meorials took on great significance for healing, as in the village of Sinitis:

> Hesperius asked us to come to his house . . . he begged us to have the sacred earth buried somewhere, and a place of prayer established on the spot, so that Christians might assemble there to celebrate the worship of God. . . . There was in that place a young rustic suffering from paralysis. When he heard what had happened he begged his parents to carry him to that sacred spot. . . . He was carried there; he prayed; and he left the place cured, on his own legs.[14]

Augustine found himself involved in relics, and Africa had long been noted for relics: "But, how about Africa: is it not full of the bodies of holy martyrs?"[15] There now seemed to be a wave of miraculous cures, some seventy in Hippo itself. In 424 a memorial was built in Hippo, by Eraclius—at his own expense—decorated with mosaics depicting the blessed saint's death, and, appropriate verses written by Augustine himself. We wonder if it might not be acquiescence on Augustine's part. To what extent did he accept miracles? He insisted on a written statement from every person claiming to have been healed, and this document was read in church, with the writer present. It was then deposited in the bishop's library. As early as 390 he had insisted that miracles, akin to those of the Apostles' time, were no longer allowed to take place.[16] Had Augustine become credulous in his later years? Hardly; he was never superstitious, and he resented crude interpretations of miracles. It would appear that he simply developed an appreciation for miracles as supportive of faith: "Such is the impressive reasoning of the wise; but 'God knows their thoughts, how futile they are.' " He continues:

> It is beyond dispute that on sober and rational consideration the interweaving of material with immaterial substances proves to be a greater miracle of divine power than the conjunction of the material with the material, different though they may be in that the one is heavenly and the other terrestrial.[17]

The years 424 and 425 found Augustine completing *City of God* and bringing *On Christian Doctrine* to fulfillment. Numerous local problems at Hippo did not keep him from preaching. His people anxiously awaited his sermons, for these were perilous times; an ancient terror clutched human hearts. In Spain the Vandals looked with larcenous eyes on the wealth of Africa—a treasure to be seized. How could Augustine best serve his people during these stormy times? Preaching, of course; but what of administration? He had a plan.

Augustine took action almost identical to that of of old Valerius, back in 395; in fact that is where the idea originated. On September 26, 426, Augustine gathered his clergy in the Basilica of Peace and, amid a huge congregation, nominated Eraclius as his successor:

> After Bishop Augustine had seated himself on his throne . . . [he] spoke thus . . . 'In this life we are all mortal men and the last day of this life is always uncertain for every man. In infancy our hopes are fixed on childhood, in childhood we look to adolescence, in adolescence we look forward to manhood, in manhood to middle age, in middle age to old age. Whether this will be our lot we do not know, but it is what we hope for. . . . God willed that I should come to this city in the vigor of manhood, but I have now passed through middle age and have reached old age.

When Augustine announced, "I want the priest Eraclius for my successor," the people thundered, "Thanks be to God" some twenty three times. They also added, sixteen times, "Long life to Augustine!" And then, eight times, to Augustine, "You are our father, you our bishop!"[18]

Having been thus confirmed, the successor preached as Augustine sat on his throne. Eraclius had the wit to observe, "The cricket chirps; the swan is silent."[19] Now there would be more time for people—or would there?

Severus of Milevis had died earlier in the year and Augustine travelled to Milevis to regulate the succession, for who else could handle all things so well? He was a legend in his own time; a cosmic authority. "Under bishop Augustine, everyone who lives with him, lives the life described in the Acts of the Apostles."[20] Many regarded him as too strict. A scandal had come to light in 424. One of his clergy had failed to donate all personal property to the church. Upon his death, the heirs were bickering over the estate. Augustine handled the matter judiciously. Obviously the priest had lied, but perhaps the rules *were* overly strict. "Look," exclaimed Augustine, "before the eyes of God and you all, I changed my mind. Whoever wants private means, whoever is not satisfied with God and his Church, let him reside where he wants: I will not deprive him of his holy orders. I do not want any hypocrites. . . . If he is prepared to live off God through his Church, and to have nothing of his own . . . let him stay with me. Whoever does not want this, let him have his freedom: but he shall see for himself whether he can have his eternal happiness." As he went on, Augustine spoke as one become tired. This ignominy had wounded, and there was anguish:

> I have spoken a lot: please forgive me. I am a long-winded old man, and ill-health has made me anxious. As you see, I have grown old with the passing years; but, for a long time now, this ill-health has made an old man of me. But, if God is pleased with what I have just said, He will give me strength: I will not desert you.[21]

He now stipulated that in the future, anyone who pretended to have willed money to the church, and lied, would be degraded at once. "Let him appeal to a thousand councils against me, let him sail to court wherever he wants, let him do what he can, when he can: God will help me; where I am bishop, he will not be priest."[22] Augustine carefully stipulated the need for a precise account of the financial holdings of each of his priests, even to personal clothing: and Augustine was the first to comply.

Always the writer, Augustine completed *On Grace and Free Will* and *Admonition and Grace* in 426, and then, *mirabile dictu,* undertook the review of all his writings, and the following year published his famous *Retractions.* It is amazing that a man of his age, burdened with heavy responsibilities, would review his voluminous writings, make corrections and additions, give a critique, and carefully catalogue the titles, arranging them in chronological order. He was a man of integrity. That same year, 427, he also wrote *Against Maximinus* and his *Two Letters to Quodvultdeus.*

During these years, Augustine composed his brief *In Answer to the Jews,* a compassionate message, in which he seems to be calling for understanding by all: an irenic treatise.

> Dearly beloved, whether the Jews receive these divine testimonies with joy or with indignation, nevertheless, when we can, let us proclaim them with great love for the Jews. Let us not proudly glory against the broken branches; let us rather reflect by whose grace it is, and by much mercy, and on what root, we have been ingrafted. Then, not savoring of pride, but with a deep sense of humility, not insulting with presumption, but rejoicing with trembling, let us say: "Come ye and let us walk in the light of the Lord," because His "name is great among the Gentiles."[23]

In 428 Augustine received letters from admirers in southern Gaul, Prosper and Hilary, asking about motivation for becoming priests and monks. There was a resurgence of faith, and many were turning to the church for vocational outlet. In Africa there was another spirit, for in May of 429 a seemingly boundless army of Genseric's Vandals crossed from Spain and slowly marched across Mauretania,[24] and lecherously ravaged Numidia the following year. It was a time such as "would make the soul shudder." Ferocious legions were brutalizing Africa. Augustine wrote to Boniface, expressing his alarm and urging the Count to bestir himself: this was no time for feckless indolence.

> What shall I say of the ravaging of Africa, which is being carried on by African barbarians with no one to oppose them as long as you are so absorbed in your own difficulties that you take not steps to ward off the disaster? Who would have believed, who would have feared that the barbarians could have dared so much, advanced so far, ravaged so widely, looted so much property, made a desert of so many places which had been thickly peopled, when Boniface had been appointed Count of the Household of Africa, with so great an army and with such power, whereas while a tribune, with a few provincial forces, he had subdued all these tribes by aggressive and repressive measures?[25]

In the face of such contiguous peril, why the lethargy?

What does one preach amid such a crisis, with the old fear of lapse as the faithful saw a real possibility of persecution, massacre, torture? As the Vandals closed in on Hippo, Augustine prayed he and his flock might persevere:

> When the good and wicked suffer alike, the identity of their sufferings does not mean that there is no difference between them. . . . Virtue and vice are not the same, even if they undergo the same torment. The fire which makes gold shine makes chaff smoke; the same flail breaks up the straw, and clears the grain; and oil is not mistaken for lees because both are forced out by the same press. . . . Thus the wicked, under pressure of affliction, execrate God and blaspheme; the good . . . offer up prayers and praises. . . . Stir a cesspit, and a foul stench arises; stir a perfume, and a delightful fragrance ascends.[26]

It is not surprising that during the long months of 428 and 429 Augustine was writing *On the Predestination of the Saints* and *On the Gifts of Perseverance*. What, now, about Christian commitment? A "gift of perseverance" was God's greatest donation to an individual. Augustine told his shaken flock, during the early months of 430, they must "persevere" in Christ. Crowds were panic-stricken; for them predestination was a doctrine of survival. God alone would provide the faithful with strength and courage.[27] He alone was their mainstay.

It is well Augustine offered support in the spiritual realm, for the government did nothing of a military nature. Roman rule collapsed in Africa; only three cities remained in their hands: Carthage, Cirta, Hippo. There is no record of resistance to the Vandals—a horde numbering a possible eighty thousand. Augustine ordered all bishops to stay by their flocks.

A great many Catholic bishops suddenly lost all taste for martyrdom. Their ardor for evangelism disappeared, and the Donatists laughed at them, saying the Catholics had never been a church of martyrs, and they were now proving it. "If we have to stay in our churches," wrote one demoralized Catholic bishop, "I do not see what good we can do for ourselves or for our people; it will be nothing but men being killed, women violated, churches burned, and ourselves fainting under torture when we are asked for what we have not." Augustine's reply was implicit: "If anyone flees in such wise as to withdraw from the flock of Christ the nourishment necessary for their spiritual life, he is a hireling 'who sees the wolf coming and flees because he has no care for the sheep'. . . . Some prudent and holy men have won merit by the grace of God by doing this very thing, that is, not forsaking their churches, and have stood against the teeth of their detractors without the least diminution of their strength of purpose."[28]

Hippo's fortifications were meager, and who should be in charge of the small garrison but the great Boniface himself, now severely limited in power but conducting himself admirably as a good soldier. Winter of 430 saw Vandals surround the town and their fleet blockade the harbor. It was all coming home to him; Augustine had once described the macabre siege of Saguntum: "In the midst of all the horrors of the Second Punic War . . . to read of its end fills one with horror. . . . If the people of Saguntum had been Christians?" Now Christians *were* besieged and it lasted fourteen months and ended in fire. Two Catholic bishops had been tortured to death outside their captured towns. When, and how, would the end come for Hippo?

> The man of God saw whole cities sacked, country villas razed, their owners killed or scattered as refugees, the churches deprived of their bishops and clergy, and the holy virgins and ascetics dispersed; some tortured to death, some killed outright, others, as prisoners, reduced to losing their integrity, in soul and body, to serve an evil and brutal enemy. The hymns of God and praises in the churches has come to a stop; in many places, the church-buildings were burnt to the ground; the sacrifices of God could no longer be celebrated in their proper place, and the

divine sacraments were either not sought, or, when sought, no one could be found to give them.[29]

Augustine waited in Hippo. It was his library that claimed his attention. In the little cupboards, on shelves, there were ninety-three of his own works—made up of two hundred and thirty-two little books, sheafs of his letters, and covers filled with anthologies of his sermons, taken down by stenographers. Some manuscripts were in need of editing, some were incomplete drafts.[30] There were précis of works. Many outlines he had permitted to be copied before the work was in final form. So Augustine worked among his books until the time of his death —setting his library in order, with patrician calm and dignity.

Augustine had one regret about his work in the library: the effort against Julian prevented his giving more time to a commentary on his letters and his sermons. His colleagues urged him on in his endeavor. They saw that in years to come the church would need Augustine's work as the norm. In an uncertain future, his books assumed increased value.

Augustine did not permit outside belligerence to deter his preaching, and what a theme! His messages now reflected a beautiful love of life. Of the martyrs he said: "They really loved this life; yet they weighed it up. They thought of how much they should love the things eternal; if they were capable of so much love for things that pass away."

And to his own flock:

> I know you want to keep on living. You do not want to die. And you want to pass from this life to another in such a way that you will not rise again, as a dead man, but fully alive and transformed. This is what you desire. This is the deepest human feeling: mysteriously, the soul itself wishes and instinctively desires it.[31]

In August, 430 Augustine fell ill with fever. He knew he was about to die and now, he who demanded human fellowship all his life, *wished to be absolutely alone!* "When it is well with a man, the Christian is left to himself," he had said. Visitors were permitted only at special times—when his meals were served. Nothing must interrupt his prayers and his thoughts: "lest his attention be distracted . . . almost

ten days before his death, he asked that none should come to see him,
except at those hours when the doctors would come to examine him or
his meals were brought. This was duly observed: and so he had all that
stretch of time to pray." What were the thoughts which clustered now?
Memories? And what of the faces? The loving mistress, Monica, Adeodatus, Ambrose, the nameless friend, his fellow priests and bishops
who were long gone from this life—did he think of them now? Were
they expunged from his memory?

> Whoever does not want to fear, let him probe his inmost self.
> Do not just touch the surface; go down into yourself; reach into
> the farthest corner of your heart. Examine it then with care: see
> there, whether a poisoned vein of the wasting love of the world
> still does not pulse, whether you are not moved by some physi-
> cal desires, and are not caught in some new law of the senses;
> whether you are never elated with empty boasting, never de-
> pressed by some vain anxiety: then only can you dare to an-
> nounce that you are pure and crystal clear when you have sifted
> everything in the deepest recesses of your inner being.[32]

Traditionally, Augustine is supposed to have chosen the seven penitential psalms (Possidius says "the very brief penitential psalms of
David") and had them copied and hung on his walls, "he could see
these sheets of paper every day, . . . and would read them, crying constantly and deeply."[33] It was much later—possibly not until the time of
Gregory the Great—the psalms were related to the seven deadly sins:
pride (from which all other sins flow)—Psalm 32. "Pride," he once
wrote, "is the mother of these maladies."[34] The list: envy—Psalm
130; anger—Psalm 6; sloth—Psalm 143; avarice—Psalm 102; glut-
tony—Psalm 38; lust—Psalm 51. The listing is much later in history,
but the spirit and attitude of Augustine is reflected amazingly. Only
God can forgive sin, and his forgiveness is seen and understood in the
light of his grace. Man is weak, impotent, and utterly inadequate to
blot out his own transgressions.

Augustine died on August 28, 430. Prayers were being said for him
in all the churches of Hippo, especially the Basilica of Peace, during
those final hours. Possidius—Alypius is not mentioned—and two other
bishops were with him singing canticles! Suddenly his voice became
still. He was buried later that same day.

> Do you wonder that the world is failing? Wonder that the world is grown old. It is as a man, who is born, grows up, and waxes old. Many are the complaints in old age: the cough, the rheum, the bleary eyes, fretfulness and lassitude are its lot. As then a man when he is old is full of complaints, so the world when it is old is full of troubles. Is it a little thing that God has done for you, in that in the world's old age He sent Christ for you that He may restore you when all else is falling.[35]

A group of African bishops reportedly took the body of Augustine with them when they fled the Vandals, depositing it at Sardinia. Here it remained until the eighth century. At the time of the Saracen invasion, King Luitprand of Lombardy secured the body through huge payment and brought it to Pavia where it was buried. A white marble sarcophagus was discovered October 1, 1695, amid great controversy as to the actual identity of the one buried. In the old monastic church of San Pietro in Ciel d'oro at Pavia (just south of Milan, scene of his conversion) a white marble sarcophagus under a brick mausoleum contains a silver chest. Supposedly here rest the mortal remains of Augustine.[36]

A Man

Usually referred to as a—some would say *the*—great Doctor of the Latin Church, Augustine holds one of the highest positions, not only in the Roman Catholic tradition, but in the entire Christian fellowship. He was a foremost theologian, a writer of tremendous depth. His place in Western history is secure.

It is said that Augustine's progressive and continuing criticisms of himself—throughout his life—were criticisms and evaluations of the cultural aspects of the ancient world in which he lived. He passed from Vergil and Cicero to Plotinus and Porphyry, and from these philosophers to the biblical and dogmatic viewpoint of his mature years. He well-nigh determined the culture of Western Christianity. He assuredly dominated the early Middle Ages. How extraordinary that a fourth and fifth century African would establish life-thought patterns which prevailed throughout almost the whole of Medieval Europe. He was father of the Christian Culture which produced Charlemagne, Innocent III, and Thomas Aquinas.

During the twelfth and thirteenth centuries Augustine's interpretation of Plato greatly influenced the church. His writings were used by the humanists of the Renaissance. Luther and Calvin turned to his theology and made wide use of it. As a puritan, Augustine's concepts—so carefully prayed through and lucidly written—were expounded in Hippo. Centuries later these same views would bear rich fruit in Geneva, Edinburgh, Westminster, and Boston. When the Spanish established their first permanent settlement in Florida in 1565 they named it for Augustine. In the seventeenth century, Descartes and Pascal drew philosophical inspiration from him. It would be impossible to estimate the number of individuals who have turned to him for inspiration, as in Thomas Coke's reading of Augustine during his first voyage to America in 1784. Augustine's influence became widespread again during the twentieth century. All this we know. But do we remember him as a man?

We have attempted to see Augustine as a person, an African, a man of flesh and blood. He was a vivid personality. He lived deeply; he was one who possessed strong emotions and he expressed forceful inner feelings. He was intensely human. As a youth he sinned with abandon; he likewise wept with equal freedom as he prayed to be forgiven. Not always beneficent in the manner whereby he responded to his opposition, he could be compassionate and forgiving; he could be loving. He knew laughter and tears; joy and sorrow; health and illness; pleasure and pain.

Augustine lived a long full life. He was very much a man.

> God loves us such as we shall be; not such as we are. . . . But by what merit, except that of faith, by which we believe before we see that which is promised? For by this faith we shall attain to sight; that He may love us such as He loves that we may be, not such as He hates, because we are; and He exhorts us and gives it to us to wish that we may not always be.[37]

Augustine's day in the lexicon of Roman Catholic saints, is August 28. Official canonization through councils of the Roman Church did not begin until the tenth century. Prior to that time the honor of sainthood was often—if not usually—bestowed by popular acclaim. By the sixth century the term had become a designation of honor applied exclusively to those whose public veneration was approved by the church. Perhaps this would be the most appropriate means to honor Augustine, through public expression. He was one who lived among people, and he prayed, "And when you pour yourself out over us, you are not drawn down to us but draw us up to yourself; you are not scattered away, but you gather us together."[38] Again, "You who hear my confessions and forgive me my sins command me to love my neighbour as myself,. . . we are all made from the same clay and man is nothing unless you remember him."[39]

Notes

Chapter I

1 See Father Hugh Pope, *Saint Augustine of Hippo* (Westminster, Maryland: The Newman Press, 1949), pp. 2-4, to whom the author is indebted for this splendid outline of the story of Roman Africa.
2 Ibid.
3 *City of God*, 1.
4 David Knowles, ed., *Augustine: The City of God* (Middlesex, England, Penguin Books, Ltd., 1972) p. vii.
5 *On the Psalms*, 120.

Chapter II

1 See Jacques Chabannes, *St. Augustine*, trans. Julie Kernan (Garden City, N.Y.: Doubleday & Co., Inc., 1962), p. 9.
2 Letter 7; see also Peter Brown, *Augustine of Hippo* (Berkeley & Los Angeles: University of California Press, 1967), p. 20.
3 See Louis Bertrand, *Saint Augustin*, trans. Vincent O'Sullivan (London: Constable & Co., 1914), p. 14.
4 *On the Magnitude of the Soul*, 21.
5 Letter 91.
6 Letter 199.
7 Letter 55.
8 *Against the Academics*, 2.
9 Letter 7.
10 *Confessions*, 10.
11 Ibid., 4.
12 Chabannes, p. 11.
13 See Gerald Bonner, *St. Augustine of Hippo* (Philadelphia: The Westminster Press, 1963), p. 37.
14 *Confessions*, 2.
15 See Chabannes, p. 12.
16 Sermon 356.
17 *Confessions*, 1.
18 Ibid., 2.
19 Ibid., 9.
20 Ibid.
21 See Bonner, p. 38.
22 *Confessions*, 9.
23 Ibid.

Chapter III

1 Possidius, *Life of Augustine*, 26. See also Bonner, p. 40.
2 *Confessions*, 1.
3 Ibid.
4 *City of God*, 21.
5 *Confessions*, 1.
6 Letter 17.
7 *Confessions*, 1.
8 Ibid.
9 Ibid., 12.
10 Ibid., 5.
11 Ibid., 10.
12 Letter 29.
13 *City of God*, 8.
14 Letter 138.
15 *Confessions*, 1.
16 Ibid.
17 Ibid., 2.
18 Ibid.
19 *On Genesis*, 10. See also Brown, p. 172.

Chapter IV

1 *Confessions*, 3.
2 *City of God*, 1.
3 *On the Happy Life*, 4.
4 *Confessions*, 3.
5 Ibid.
6 Ibid.
7 Ibid.
8 Ibid.
9 Ibid.
10 Ibid.
11 *On the Psalms*, 36.
12 Sermon 270.
13 See Brown, p. 45.; also pp. 46-56.
14 *Confessions*, 3.
15 Ibid.
16 *On the Value of Believing*, 17.
17 Ibid., 1.
18 *Against Faustus, the Manichaean*, 21.
19 Ibid., 1.
20 *On the Two Souls*, II, cited in Brown, p. 48.
21 Sermon 17.

22 *Confessions*, 4.
23 Ibid., 6.
24 See Pope, p. 92, who insists: "Nowhere does Augustine anywhere suggest that he was in love with his mistress, though he does say that he was always faithful to her."
25 *On the Good of Marriage*, 5.
26 *Soliloquies*, 1.
27 *Confessions*, 9.

Chapter V

1 *Confessions*, 3.
2 Ibid.
3 Ibid.
4 Ibid., 4.
5 Ibid.
6 *Confessions*, 1, variant translation.
7 *Against Faustus, the Manichaean*, 13.
8 *Confessions*, 4.
9 Ibid., 6.
10 Ibid.
11 Ibid.
12 *Against the Academics.*
13 *Confessions*, 6.
14 Ibid., 4.
15 Letter 98.
16 Letter 3.
17 *Confessions*, 9.
18 Letter 5, Nebridius to Augustine.
19 *Confessions*, 9.
20 *Concerning Faith of Things Unseen*, 40.
21 Sermon 341.
22 *On Catechizing the Uninstructed*, 1.
23 *On the Morals of the Catholic Church*, 1.
24 *Confessions*, 4.
25 Ibid.
26 Ibid., 3.
27 Ibid.
28 Ibid., 4.
29 Quoted in Brown, p. 66.
30 *Confessions*, 7.
31 Ibid., 4.
32 Ibid.
33 Ibid.
34 Ibid.

35 Ibid., 5.
36 Ibid.
37 Ibid.
38 Ibid.
39 *On the Trinity*, 8.
40 Ibid., 9.

Chapter VI

1 *Confessions*, 5.
2 Ibid.
3 *Sermon on the First Epistle of Saint John*, 5.
4 *On the Trinity*, 2.
5 *Confessions*, 5.
6 Ibid.
7 *Against the Academics*, 3.
8 *Confessions*, 5.
9 Ibid.
10 Ambrose, Letter 28.
11 *Confessions*, 5.
12 Ibid., 6.
13 *On the Morals of the Catholic Church* and *On the Morals of the Manichaeans*, 1.
14 *Confessions*, 6.
15 Ibid.
16 Ibid.
17 Ibid., 9.
18 Ibid., 6.
19 Ibid.
20 Letter 167 of Pope Leo, cited in Brown, p. 88.
21 *Confessions*, 6.
22 Ibid., 8.
23 *On the Good of Marriage*, 6.
24 *On Holy Virginity*, 55.
25 *Confessions*, 6.
26 Ibid.
27 Ibid.
28 *Against the Academics*, 3.
29 *City of God*, 18.
30 Ibid., 10.
31 Ibid.
32 Ibid.
33 *Soliloquies*, 1.
34 *Confessions*, 8.
35 Ibid.

36 Ibid., 7.
37 *Against the Academics*, 3.
38 Ambrose, Letter 34, cited in Brown, p. 93.
39 *Confessions*, 4.
40 Ibid., 7.
41 Ibid.
42 Ibid.
43 *City of God*, 10.
44 *On the Psalms*, 38.
45 *Admonition and Grace*, 12.
46 *Retractions*, 1:8.

Chapter VII

1 *Confessions*, 8.
2 Ibid.
3 Ibid.
4 Romano Guardini, *The Conversion of Augustine*, trans. Elinor Briefs (Westminster, Maryland: Newman Press, 1960), p. 242.
5 *Confessions*, 9.
6 Ibid., 8.
7 Ibid., 9.
8 *On the Psalms*, 129.
9 *On the Trinity*, 4.
10 *Confessions*, 9.
11 Ibid.
12 Ibid.
13 Bertrand, p. 225.
14 *Against the Academics*, 2.
15 Ibid., 1.
16 Letter 1.
17 *Retractions*, 1:2.
18 *On the Happy Life*, 1.
19 Ibid., 4.
20 *Retractions*, 1:3.
21 *On Order*, 1.
22 Ibid.
23 Ibid., 20.
24 Letter 2.
25 *Retractions*, 1:4.
26 *Soliloquies*, 1.
27 Ibid., 2.
28 *Confessions*, 9.
29 *Retractions*, 1:11.
30 *Confessions*, 9.

31 *On the Teacher*, 1.
32 Ibid., 3.
33 *Confessions*, 9.
34 *Retractions*, 1:5.
35 *Soliloquies*, 2.
36 *On the Immortality of the Soul*, 1.
37 Ibid.
38 Ibid., 5.
39 Ibid., 8.
40 Ibid., 16.
41 *Retractions*, 1:10.
42 *On Music*, 1.
43 Ibid., 6.
44 Ibid., 17.
45 *Confessions*, 13.
46 *City of God*, 15 (paraphrase).
47 *On Christian Doctrine*, 3.
48 *Confessions*, 9.
49 Ibid., 13.
50 Ibid., 9.
51 *City of God*, 22; see also *Confessions*, 9.
52 *Confessions*, 9.
53 *Soliloquies*, 2.
54 *On the Magnitude of the Soul, 34.*
55 See Brown, p. 128.
56 *Confessions*, 9.
57 Ibid.
58 Ibid.
59 *Care for the Dead*, 2.
60 *Confessions*, 9; sometimes known as Ambrose's Evening Hymn.
61 Ibid.
62 *On Order*, 2.
63 *On the Happy Life*, 2.
64 *On the Gift of Perseverance*, 20.
65 *Retractions*, 1:7.
66 *On the Magnitude of the Soul*, 7.
67 Ibid., 36.
68 *Retractions*, 1:8.
69 Ibid., 6.
70 Sermon 36.

Chapter VIII

1 *City of God*, 22.
2 Letter 10.

3 Ibid., 6.
4 Ibid., 10.
5 *Confessions*, 9.
6 Letter 18.
7 Letter 15.
8 *Retractions*, 1:12.
9 *On True Religion*, 1.
10 Ibid.
11 Ibid., 55.
12 *On the Psalms*, 104. See Brown, pp. 277–78.
13 Sermon 355.
14 Ibid.
15 Letter 21.
16 Sermon 216.
17 Ibid., 214.
18 Letter 21.
19 Ibid.
20 *On the Value of Believing*, 1.
21 *Retractions*, 1:13.
22 *On the Value of Believing*, 1.
23 Ibid., 18.
24 *Against Fortunatus the Manichaean*, 1.
25 *Retractions*, 1:15.
26 *On Free Will*, 1.
27 *Retractions*, 1:8.
28 Letter 28.
29 *On the Psalms*.
30 *On the Lord's Sermon on the Mount*, 1.
31 *Retractions*, 1:18.
32 *On the Lord's Sermon on the Mount*, 22.
33 *Retractions*, 1:18.
34 Ibid., 1:9.
35 Ibid., 17.
36 Letter 22.
37 *Retractions*, 1:16.
38 *On the Faith and the Creed*, 1.
39 *Retractions*, 1:22.
40 Ibid., 23.
41 Bertrand, p. 315.
42 *Retractions*, 2:31.
43 Brown, p. 141.
44 Letter 110.
45 Ibid., 104.
46 Ibid., 12.
47 Ibid., 118.

48 Ibid., 174.
49 Ibid., 171.
50 Ibid., 15.
51 Ibid., 143.
52 Ibid., 6.
53 Ibid., 13.
54 Ibid., 17.
55 Ibid., 18.
56 Ibid., 23.
57 Ibid., 26.
58 Ibid., 50.
59 Ibid., 100.
60 Bertrand, p. 267.
61 Letter 38.
62 Sermon 355.
63 Sermon, *On Episcopal Ordination*.
64 See Brown, p. 11.

Chapter IX

1 Letter 22.
2 See Brown, pp. 159–61.
3 Letter 231, cited in Pope, p. 107.
4 *Confessions*, 1.
5 *Retractions*, 2:32.
6 *Confessions*, 10.
7 Ibid., 5.
8 Ibid., 11.
9 Ibid., 13.
10 *Retractions*, 2:30.
11 Ibid., 2:27.
12 Letter 174.
13 *On the Trinity*, 8.
14 Ibid.
15 *Retractions*, 2:38.
16 Ibid., 2:47.
17 Ibid., 2:33.
18 *On the Lord's Sermon on the Mount*, 1.
19 *On the Gospels*, 4.
20 *Confessions*, 10.
21 Ibid.
22 *On Various Questions to Simplicanius*, 1.
23 Ibid. Also see Brown, pp, 155–156.
24 *Against Lying*, 18.
25 Letter 99.

26 Ibid., 118.
27 Ibid., 124.
28 See Brown, p. 193.
29 Letter 122.
30 Ibid., 38.
31 Sermon 356. See Brown, p. 140.
32 From Vernon J. Bourke, *Augustine's Quest of Wisdom* (Milwaukee, Wisconsin: The Bruce Publishing Co., 1942), p. 20. Also see F. Van der Meer, *Augustine the Bishop* (London and New York: Sheed and Ward, 1961), p. 216.
33 Letter 133.
34 Ibid., 136, Marcellinus to Augustine.
35 Ibid., 78; also see Brown, p. 196.
36 Possidius, *Life of Augustine*, 26.
37 Ibid., 22.
38 *Against Julian*, 4. See also Pope, p. 134.
39 Possidius, *Life of Augustine*, 22.
40 Letter 73.
41 *Confessions*, 10.
42 *Admonition and Grace*, 15.
43 *On Christian Doctrine*, 1.
44 *Concerning Faith on Things Unseen*, 4.
45 Letter 210.
46 Ibid., 68, Jerome to Augustine.
47 Letter 73.
48 Ibid., 60.
49 *On the Trinity*, 9.
50 Letter 40.
51 Ibid., 67.
52 Ibid., 73.
53 Ibid., 110, paraphrased.
54 *Against Julian*, 5.
55 Sermon 3, from Brown, p. 402.
56 *On the Trinity*, 15.
57 Sermon 320. See also Pope, pp. 142–43.
58 Possidius, *Life of Augustine*, 15.
59 *Retractions*, 2:29.
60 *On Christian Doctrine*, 4.
61 See Chabannes, p. 136.
62 *Treatise on the Punishment and Remission of Sin* 1:24.
63 Sermon 252.
64 See Brown, p. 416.
65 Sermon 272.
66 Letter 22.
67 Ibid., 29. See Bonner, pp. 116–17, and Brown, p. 207.

68 Letter 23.
69 Ibid., 34.
70 *On the Psalms*, 3.
71 *Against Parmenian*, 3. See also Brown, p. 228.
72 *Against Gaudentius*, 19. See Brown, p. 238.
73 *Concerning Faith on Things Unseen.*
74 Letter 141.
75 *Against Lying*, 3.
76 *On the Position of the Pelagians*, 25.
77 See Brown, p. 342.
78 Pelagius, *Letter to Demetrius*, 2, from Brown, p. 342.
79 Letter 145.
80 *On Nature and Grace*, 29.
81 Sermon 174.
82 *Confessions*, 1.
83 Ibid., 4.
84 Pelagius, *To Demetrius*, 17; Brown, p. 352.
85 *On Grace and Free Will*, 6.
86 Sermon 162.
87 *The Spirit and the Letter.*
88 Letter 177.
89 Zosimus, Letter 1.
90 Letter 201, Emperors Honorius and Theodosius to Aurelius.
91 Sermon 181. See Brown, p.363.
92 *The Spirit and the Letter*, 13.
93 Ibid., 19.
94 *On Nature and Grace*, 70.
95 *Sermon on the First Epistle of Saint John*, 7, paraphrased.
96 Ibid., 5.
97 *Admonition and Grace*, 2.
98 Sermon 31.
99 *Against Julian*, 4.
100 Letter 130.
101 *Against Julian*, 3. See also Brown, p. 405.
102 *Admonition and Grace*, 9.
103 *Letters Against the Semi-Pelagians*, 3.
104 Sermon 159.
105 *Against Julian*, 6.
106 Ibid., 3; and 1.
107 Sermon 252.
108 *On the Psalms*, 149.
109 Ibid., 105.
110 Ibid., 99.
111 Sermon 130.

Chapter X

1 Sermon 55. The author is indebted to Brown, pp. 287ff. and 313ff.
2 Ibid., 105.
3 *On the Divination of Demons*, 4.
4 *On the Psalms*, 136.
5 Ibid.
6 Ibid., 64. See Brown, pp. 314–315.
7 Ibid.
8 Sermon 51.
9 *On the Psalms*, 64.
10 *Second Discourse on Psalm 25.*
11 Letter 138.
12 *City of God*, 10.
13 Letter 138.
14 *On Christian Doctrine*, 1.
15 *On the Psalms*, 29.
16 Sermon 256.
17 Letter 95.
18 Ibid.
19 Pelagius, *Letter to Demetrius*, 30. See Brown, p. 289.
20 Jerome, Letter 123. See Brown, p. 289.
21 *City of God*, 1.
22 *Retractions*, 2:69.
23 Letter 138.
24 Hans Von Campenhausen, *The Fathers of the Latin Church*, trans. Manfred Hoffmann (London: Adam & Charles Black, 1964), Chapter VI, "Augustine," p. 241.
25 Brown, p. 291.
26 Letter 140.
27 *Retractions*, 2:69.
28 See Knowles, *p. xvi.*
29 *City of God*, 15.
30 Ibid., 13.
31 Ibid., 1.
32 Ibid., 18.
33 Ibid., 19.
34 Chabannes, p. 170.
35 Letter 203.
36 *City of God*, 5.
37 Letter 118.
38 *City of God*, 10.
39 Ibid., 3.
40 Ibid., 5.
41 *On the Psalms*, 84.
42 *City of God*, 22.

Chapter XI

1 Letter 118.
2 Ibid., 140.
3 Ibid., 125.
4 Ibid., 124.
5 Ibid., 167.
6 Ibid., 151.
7 Ibid., 21.
8 Ibid., 185.
9 Ibid., 220.
10 Ibid., 209.
11 Ibid., 195, Jerome to Augustine.
12 Ibid., 263, paraphrased.
13 Possidius, *Life of Augustine*, 29.
14 *City of God*, 22.
15 Letter 78.
16 *On the True Religion*, 25. See also Brown, pp. 413–415.
17 *City of God*, 22.
18 Letter 213.
19 *Sermon of Eraclius*. See Brown, p. 408.
20 Sermon 356.
21 Sermon 355. See Brown, p. 410.
22 Sermon, 356.
23 *In Answer to the Jews*, 10.
24 See Giovanni Papini, *Saint Augustine*, trans. Mary Prichard Agnetti (New York: The Book League of America, 1930), p. 174.
25 Letter 220.
26 *City of God*, 1.
27 *On the Gifts of Perseverance*, 7.
28 Letter 228.
29 Possidius, *Life of Augustine*, 28. See also Brown, p. 428.
30 See Brown, p. 428.
31 Sermon 344. See Brown, p. 431.
32 Sermon 348. See Brown, p. 432.
33 Possidius, *Life of Augustine*, 31.
34 Letter 22.
35 Sermon 81.
36 See Pope, p. 138.
37 *On the Trinity*, 1.
38 *Confessions*, 1.
39 Ibid., 12.

Bibliography

Augustine

Admonition and Grace
An Explanation of Certain Passages of Romans
An Explanation of Galatians
An Unfinished Work Against Julian
Against Faustus, The Manichaean
Against Fortunatus
Against Gaudentius
Against Julian and the Pelagians
Against Lying
Against Maximinus
Against Parmenian
Against Pelagius and Caelestius
Against the Academics
Against the Letters of Petilianus
Beauty and Proportion
Care for the Dead
City of God
Confessions
Concerning Faith on Things Unseen
Discourse in Caesarea on Catholic Unity
Discourse on Peace
Divine Providence and the Problem of Evil
Exposition on the Book of Psalms
Four Letters to Boniface
In Answer to the Jews
Letters Against the Semi-Pelagians
Letter to Dioscorus
Letter to the Donatists
Letter to Emeritus
Letters to Jerome
Letter to Maximus of Madaura
Letters to Nebridius
Letters to Paulinus of Nola
Letter to Romanianus
Letter to Vincent the Rogatist
On the Advantages of Believing

On Catechizing of the Uninstructed
On Christian Doctrine
On the Divination of Demons
On Eighty-three Different Questions
On the Faith and the Creed
On Faith and Works
On Free Will
On Genesis
On the Gifts of Perseverance
On the Good of Marriage
On Grace and Free Will
On the Gospels
On Grammar
On Holy Virginity
On the Happy Life
On the Immortality of the Soul
On the Lord's Sermon on the Mount
On the Magnitude of the Soul
On the Manichaean Heresy
On Marriage and Concupiscence
On the Morals of the Catholic Church
On the Morals of the Manichaeans
On Music
On the Nature of Good
On Nature and Grace
On Order
On the Origin of the Soul
On the Position of the Pelagians
On the Predestination of the Saints
On Single Baptism
On the Teacher
On the Trinity
On the True Religion
On the Two Souls
On the Value of Believing
On Various Questions to Simplicianus
On the Work of Monks

Retractions

Sermons Against the Pelagians

Sermon on Episcopal Ordination

Sermon on the First Epistle of Saint
John

Sermons on the Sack of Rome

Soliloquies

The Eight Questions of Dulcitius

The Enchiridion

The First Catechetical Instruction

The Problem of Free Choice

The Spirit and the Letter

The Usefulness of Fasting

Treatise on the Punishment and
Remission of Sin

Two Letters to Olympius

Two Letters to Quodvultdeus

Translations

Baillie, John; McNeille, John T.; Van Dusen, Henry P., eds. *The Library of Christian Classics*. Philadelphia: The Westminster Press, 1953.

Deferrari, Roy Joseph, ed. *The Fathers of the Church*. Washington, D. C.: The Catholic University of America Press, 1947.

Quasten, Johannes; Burghardt, Walter J., eds. *Ancient Christian Writers*. Westminster, Maryland: The Newman Press, 1960.

Knowles, David, ed. *Augustine: The City of God*. Translated by Henry Bettenson. Middlesex, England: Penguin Books Ltd., 1972.

Pine-Coffin, R. E., tr. *Saint Augustine: Confessions*. Middlesex, England: Penguin Books Ltd., 1961.

Schaff, Philip, ed. *A Select Library of Nicene and Post-Nicene Fathers of the Christian Church*. New York: The Christian Literature Company, 1886–1900.

Secondary Sources in English

Babcock, William S. *The Christ of the Exchange: A Study in the Christology of Augustine's ENARRATIONES IN PSALMOS*. Microfilmed doctoral dissertation, Yale University, 1971. University Microfilms, Ann Arbor, Michigan.

Battenhouse, Roy W. *A Companion to the Study of St. Augustine*. New York: Oxford University Press, 1955.

Bertrand, Louis. *Saint Augustin*. Translated by Vincent O'Sullivan. London: Constable and Company Ltd., 1914.

Bonner, Gerald St. *Augustine of Hippo, Life and Controversies.* Philadelphia: The Westminster Press, 1963.

Booth, Edwin Prince. "Augustine of Thagaste," in *Five Christian Warriors.* The Quillian Lectures, Emory University, 1943, typed copy.

Bourke, Vernon J. *Augustine's Quest of Wisdom.* Milwaukee, Wisconsin: The Bruce Publishing Company, 1945.

Brown, Peter. *Augustine of Hippo.* Berkeley and Los Angeles: University of California Press, 1967.

Burnaby, John. *Amor Dei, A Study of the Religion of St. Augustine.* London: Hodder & Stoughton, 1938.

Chabannes, Jacques. *St. Augustine.* Translated by Julie Kernan. Garden City, N. Y.: Doubleday & Company, Inc. 1962.

D'Arcy, M. C. *et al. Saint Augustine.* Cleveland: The World Publishing Company, 1945.

Donnelly, Dorothy H. *Augustine and Romanitas.* Microfilmed doctoral dissertation, Graduate Theological Union, 1973. University Microfilms, Ann Arbor, Michigan.

Flood, J. M. *The Mind and Heart of Augustine.* Fresno, California: Academy Guild Press, 1960.

Greenwood, David. *Saint Augustine.* New York: Vantage Press, 1956.

Guardini, Romano. *The Conversion of Augustine.* Translated by Elinor Briefs. Westminster, Maryland: The Newman Press, 1960.

Keenan, Sister Mary Emily. *The Life and Times of St. Augustine as Revealed in His Letters.* The Catholic University of America, Patristic Studies, Vol. XLV. Washington, D. C.: The Catholic University of America, 1935.

Kevane, Eugene. *Augustine the Educator.* Westminster, Maryland: The Newman Press, 1964.

McCabe, Joseph. *Saint Augustine and His Age.* London: Duckworth and Co., 1902.

McNamara, Sister Marie Aquinas. *Friends and Friendship for Saint Augustine.* Staten Island, New York: Pauline Fathers and Brothers Society, 1964.

Meagher, Robert. *Augustine: An Introduction.* N.Y.: Harper & Row, 1979.

Monagle, John F. "Friendship in St. Augustine's Biography," *Augustinian Studies,* Vol. 2, 1971, pp. 81–92.

Mullany, Katherine F. *Augustine of Hippo*. New York: Frederick Pustet Co., 1930.

Newton, John Thomas, Jr. "Neoplatonism and Augustine's Doctrine of the Person and Work of Christ: A Study of the Philosophical Structure Underlying Augustine's Christology." Unpublished doctoral dissertation. Emory University, Atlanta, Georgia, 1969.

O'Connell, Robert J. *St. Augustine's Early Theory of Man, A.D. 386–391*. Cambridge, Massachusetts: The Belknap Press of Harvard University Press, 1968.

Papini, Giovanni. *Saint Augustine*. Translated by Mary Prichard Agnetti. New York: The Book League of America, 1930.

Polman, A. D. R. *The Word of God According to St. Augustine*. Grand Rapids, Michigan: Wm. B. Erdmans Publishing Company, 1961.

Pope, Hugh. *Saint Augustine of Hippo*. Westminster, Maryland: The Newman Press, 1949.

Portalie, Eugene. *A Guide to the Thought of Saint Augustine*. Chicago: Henry Regnery Company, 1960.

Przywara, Ernich. *An Augustine Synthesis*. New York: Sheed and Ward, 1945.

Rowe, Trevor. *St. Augustine: Pastoral Theologian*. London: Epworth Press, 1974.

TeSelle, Eugene. *Augustine the Theologian*. New York: Herder and Herder, 1970.

TeSelle, Eugene. "Rufinus the Syrian, Caelestius, Pelagius: Explorations in the Prehistory of the Pelagian Controversy," *Augustinian Studies*, Vol. 3, 1972, pp. 61–95.

Van der Meer, F. *Augustine the Bishop*. Translated by Brian Battershaw and G. R. Lamb. New York: Harper & Row, Publishers. Harper Torchbooks, 1965.

Von Campenhausen, Hans. *The Fathers of the Latin Church*. Translated by Manfred Hoffmann. London: Adam & Charles Black, 1964.

West, Rebecca. *St. Augustine*. New York: D. Appleton and Company, 1933.

Willis, Geoffrey Grimshaw. *Saint Augustine and the Donatist Controversy*. London: S.P.C.K., 1950.

Index

BR
1720   Smith.
H9
S64   Augustine His life and thought.

60791

D 8953020